HUMAN SERVICES AND THE FULL SERVICE SCHOOL

HUMAN SERVICES AND
THE FULL SERVICE SCHOOL

The Need for Collaboration

Edited by

ROBERT F. KRONICK, PH.D.

Professor
Counseling, Deafness, and Human Services
The University of Tennessee
Knoxville, Tennessee

Charles C Thomas
PUBLISHER • LTD.
SPRINGFIELD • ILLINOIS • U.S.A.

Published and Distributed Throughout the World by

CHARLES C THOMAS • PUBLISHER, LTD.
2600 South First Street
Springfield, Illinois 62704

© 2000 by CHARLES C THOMAS • PUBLISHER, LTD.

ISBN 0-398-07063-6

Library of Congress Catalog Card Number: 00-022062

With THOMAS BOOKS *careful attention is given to all dtails of manufacturing
and design. It is the Publisher's desire to present books that are satisfactory as to their
physical qualities and artistic possiblities and appropriate for their particular use.*
THOMAS BOOKS *will be true to those laws of quality that assure a good name
and good will.*

Printed in the United States of America
R-3

Library of Congress Cataloging-in-Publication Data

Kronick, Robert F.
Human services and the full service school/edited by Robert F. Kroncik.
     p. cm.
Includes bibliographical references and index.
ISBN 0-398-07063-6 (paper)
1. School social work--United States. 2. Community and school--United States. 3.
Socially handicapped children--Services for--United States. I. Kronick, Robert F.
LB3013.4. H86 2000

00-022062

This book is dedicated to Joy Dryfoos and her devotion to the full service school, to the Tennessee Consortium for the Development of Full Service Schools for the nurturance which it has provided me, and to my wife Sandra and our children, Julia and Will. I have learned from you all.

Published and Distributed Throughout the World by

CHARLES C THOMAS · PUBLISHER, LTD.
2600 South First Street
Springfield, Illinois 62794

© 2000 by CHARLES C THOMAS · PUBLISHER, LTD.

ISBN 0-398-07063-6

Library of Congress Catalog Card Number: 00-032662

With THOMAS BOOKS careful attention is given to all details of manufacturing
and design. It is the Publisher's desire to present books that are satisfactory as to
physical qualities and artistic possibilities and appropriate for their particular use.
THOMAS BOOKS will be true to those laws of quality that assure a good name
and good will.

Printed in the United States of America
R-3

Library of Congress Cataloging-in-Publication Data

Kronick, Robert F.
Human services and the full service school / edited by Robert F. Kronick.
p. cm.
Includes bibliographical references and index.
ISBN 0-398-07063-6 (paper)
1. School social work–United States. 2. Community and school–United States. 3.
Socially handicapped children–Services for–United States. I. Kronick, Robert F.
LB3013.4 .H86 2000
00-032662

CONTRIBUTORS

Lisa Bloom
Joy Dryfoos
John Habel
Robert Kronick
Rebecca Lucas
Jerome Morton
Dorothy Stulberg

PREFACE

A FULL SERVICE SCHOOL is a school that has broadened its mission and vision to meet the needs of all of its students. The school is where health, mental health, and other services are provided. The emphasis is on prevention. The full service school is a new environment where a systems approach to change is used. It is not a school where human services is an add on. Collaboration thus becomes a key process in the school. Input from the community determines what special services will be provided. By meeting the non-curricular needs of children and families the full service school ensures that learning will happen for all students in the school.

R.F.K.

INTRODUCTION

THIS BOOK IS INSPIRED BY JOY DRYFOOS and her writings. I met Joy in April 1998 in San Diego, California at the American Educational Research Association annual meeting. One year later Joy gave a lecture on full service schools at the University of Tennessee, Knoxville. Her lecture inspired many in attendance to collaborate in establishing full service schools in Tennessee. Her lecture in November 1998 helped inspire the development of a group of human service professionals, educators, and students to form the Tennessee Consortium for the Development of Full Service Schools.

This group has had several notable accomplishments since its inception in December 1998. The Consortium helps school systems apply for twenty-first century after school program grants. The Consortium helped develop a handbook on how to develop full service schools. Several papers have been presented at regional and national meetings by members of the Consortium on the concept of full service schools. Finally, my special education class has been recast where the full service school is a centerpiece of the course. Thus, theory and practice have been shaped by the full service school concept. All of these issues are presented and discussed in detail in the text.

The full service schools allow teachers to teach by addressing the non-curricular needs of children and families that attend that school. It is the children and families of the school that shape the services that will be provided by the school. As a general rule, the full service school will have extended hours of operation. Programs offered may include counseling, quilt making, and providing laundry services.

In talking to children and families of the schools, we must think in non-traditional ways. The voices of children and families must be heard. What they say must shape what the school provides. The bottom line is that the full service school wants to see that all children are served. Evaluation must be done to see if full service schools are any different from traditional schools. Criterion variables would include attendance, learning as determined from qualitative interviews of teachers, test scores, and health and mental health well-being.

The school will meet the most basic needs of the children and families. These needs must be met if the child is to learn. Knowledge of human development will also be a driving force in the philosophy of the school. Developmentally appropriate behavior will be acknowledged within the school. A key desired outcome will be increased learning. The goal is that the full service school will make teaching easier. From a curricular perspective the full service school may emphasize individualized instruction because it is in concert with the non-curricular philosophy of a full service school. As one of my closest colleagues continually reminds me, the full service school will not fix all our problems. Even if we get them established on a system-wide basis, we will still have problems. Of course he is correct!

Nonetheless, from 25 years experience in corrections, I am convinced that the school is where one must do prevention and intervention. After all, that's where the children and families are. By the time these young people get into corrections it is too late for any meaningful behavioral change. We must catch these at-risk children earlier and provide them with services that for a variety of reasons they do not receive. We must set aside politics. We must think outside the "box." Curricular and non-curricular service providers must collaborate.

It is no longer a question whether the school will be a parent or not, it is, will it be a good parent!

ACKNOWLEDGMENT

I would like to thank Karen Welch Tuck
for typing this manuscript.

CONTENTS

HUMAN SERVICES AND THE FULL SERVICE SCHOOL

Chapter 1

HUMAN SERVICES: THE NEED

TODAY IS WEDNESDAY, APRIL 21, 1999. I am on my way to the American Educational Research Association Conference in Montreal, Canada. The horrible shootings at Columbine School in Littleton, Colorado happened yesterday. I can think of little else. News of the shootings is everywhere. Television and print media cover the story in gory detail. My wife and son took me to the airport. Our daughter did not get home from school in time to come to the airport. She forgot her lunch today so I took it to her at school. There were police and fire trucks in front of the school when I got there. All kinds of thoughts ran through my head fueled by the events of the prior day at Littleton. I ran into the school carrying her lunch in a Kroger bag. Everything is okay. As I leave the office the new principal of the school is in front of the door. I open the door and he doesn't move. I finally say excuse me and walk between him and the assistant principal. I fear his management style is going to lead to trouble at the school. He appears to have little if any personal contact with students or staff. His style with faculty is officious. He has a very fine faculty. I am not sure why he takes the approach he does. I want him to read *Unowned Places and Times: Maps and Interviews About Violence in High Schools* (1999). I also want him to read this book.

I want our paper to be useful in making schools more familial for all students, but especially for at-risk students, who so badly need someone to know their names, their lives,

3

their stories. Schools need to be good parents. I will be a more critical listener of other papers also.

Last night I reviewed cases for the Department of Children Services in Knoxville. Our job is to support case managers or come up with placements for their children. Every case did not have a workable home for the child. One mother was told by her boyfriend, "It's the kid or me." She chose the boyfriend.

We continue to decry the status of families in America today. This experience of working with Department of Children's Services counselors let me see up close and personal the state of some families in our area. The families of these children are in trouble. Albeit these are mostly poor families. The situation in Colorado illustrates that families rich or poor, need help in America today. The experience with the Department of Children's Services in Knoxville, Tennessee illustrates that these children need help. They are clearly at risk for a myriad of behaviors that include alcohol and drug use, violent crime, and depression. They also are likely to start their own families prematurely. After twenty-eight years in this business, this is still difficult to accept.

There is a hue and cry throughout the land over today's families. Not only do we have young poor girls having children and raising them by themselves, we also have, as illustrated above, families who throw away their children.

CHILDREN AND FAMILIES, NOT Y2K, MUST BECOME THE ISSUE OF CONCERN AND ACTION FOR THE YEAR 2000

What goes on at school? Bill Clinton stated in a speech to the American Federation of Teachers:

> Our progress will come to nothing if our schools are not safe places, orderly places, where our teachers can teach,

and children can learn. We also know that in too many American schools there is lawlessness where there should be learning. There is chaos where there should be concern. There is disorder where there should be discipline. Make no mistake this is a threat not to our classroom but to America's public school system and indeed to the strength and vitality of our nation.

What are schools doing to engender and/or exacerbate this situation? Listen to this teacher. "I can't make anything happen here. I have no power, the janitor, the secretaries, they have more power than I do. I don't have any power. There is nothing I can do. I have no voice (Astor, Meyer, and Behre, 1999, p.25).

It appears that the personal touch, now more than ever, is called for in America's schools and communities. A partial answer may lie within community or full service schools (Dryfoos 1994). I will say more of this later.

THE IMPORTANCE OF THE HUMAN SERVICE PHILOSOPHY

Human Services now more than ever, are needed by American society. What are the values and beliefs of human services? 1) People have problems in living. They should not be seen as problem people. Too often teachers and human service workers focus on peoples deficits rather than their strengths. The Appalachian child knows the beauty of the seasons, the mountains, and the streams. The migrant child knows geography, if not English quite as well. Listen to this teacher. "I think if you've got no hope, if you're surrounded by despair, then you don't see that following the rules, that good work, and good deeds will get you anywhere. The kids are pretty frank about saying, You know you're stupid if you play by the rules" (female teacher,

(Astor, Meyer, and Behre, 1999, p. 26).

If people have problems in living then it automatically follows that the helping method of choice would be one of problem-solving. By definition a problem-solving approach is short-term. This approach, though valuable in many instances, may not be ideal for the children and families of Littleton, Colorado. This illustrates that no one method will work with all problems. The method should be selected so that it fits the problem rather than forcing the problem into the method that is available. A problem-solving approach to helping will ensure that the clients will actively participate in the helping process and facilitate greater long-term change. Hence, though it may appear contradictory, we are finding that a method that is short-term in focus but problem centered will lead to greater long-term change.

In returning to the Littleton shootings, I fear that we will look for pathology within the individuals, the known shooters, and others who have helped in this process. I believe we will be better served by listening to the voices of the children and families who have gone through this ordeal to see how we might prevent such horrific disasters in the future.

It is clear that the shooters felt that they did not fit in any of the groups within their school, i.e., jocks, prom crowd, et al., so they created their own group, the Goths-the Trenchcoat Mafia. Their values were widely known. These values had to come from their families and/or their communities. These values didn't spring up from nowhere; they didn't grow in a vacuum. These values led to thoughts and actions. They appear to have been germinating for quite some time. Metal detectors and police would not and will not prevent this. What will? I believe smaller classes and the integration of human service workers into the schools are at least a beginning in making our schools safer places in which to learn. I believe a full service or community school model, in which human services are site-based or colocated is a step in the right direction. It is important to remember that marginalized people lack a sense of community and do not have a stake in conformity. When this is the case, we can expect violent eruption in people's behavior. This situation translates quite simply to when you have nothing you have nothing to lose. We must work to see that all people participate in the give and take of American society. We need to make social structures open to all people. People should not be denied access to the rewards of American society because of their age, race, gender, religion, or socioeconomic background; 2) there must be an interdisciplinary approach to teaching and learning. The issues confronting teachers, human service workers, and their students and clients today are so involved that no one discipline can prepare human service workers and teachers for their jobs and life's work. This requires a change within the academy. One that is coming, but I fear too slowly, is that academic disciplines that prepare students for teaching and the helping professions must learn to listen to each other. We must take heart from the "Noah Principle," quit predicting the weather and build the boat.

Communication and trust are the two big variables here. Jargon, the use of language that sets us apart as a profession, must be done away with. Our job is to demystify. Our profession(s) are set up in such a way that trust is difficult to establish. We must move to a position where, "What's in it for me" disappears and the benefits of teamwork outweigh the costs.

I am sure that the caseworker who gave the Littleton shooters a positive release after their community service and apology did all he could do. Yet is there something in the academic world that could have prepared him/her for this almost impossible job? Possibly more interdisciplinary education and training involving psychology, sociology, health, economics, political science, human services, and theology.

This is a daunting task but the price at Littleton and other prior cities shows that it must be done. If Littleton, then anywhere! As a community, Littleton looks like the last place where this could happen. Upon closer scrutiny, I believe we will find some strong structural barriers to full participation in the good life by all in Littleton. As in every community, there is some racism and prejudice against other groups. A hard look into the community will probably yield some fruitful answers. This in no way removes individual responsibility, but rather places it firmly within a family community context; and 3) a coordinated welfare system, broadly defined is a critical need. Clients fall through the cracks today as much as ever before. A coordinated system in which boundaries are broken down and turf issues are blown away will make the human service-education system more effective. If the interdisciplinary education is effective, coordinated services should flow naturally. Prevention at the elementary school must be our beginning point. Prevention has been a prickly issue because it has no immediate results. Yet, now more than ever, prevention must move to the forefront in our society and in our educational institutions. If school counselors and human service workers are integrated into the school, then tragedies years in the future may be prevented. Eric Harris and Dylan Klebold may have been caught in elementary school if these programs had been in place. Since they had some involvement with the human service system where they did community service and made an apology, there may have been some earlier signs that these boys were at risk.

A problem-centered focus works well within the fabric of a full service school. It also is a good fit with the philosophy of prevention. It is sad that the Littleton, Colorado crisis has not aroused a greater concern for prevention than it has. The only responses heard have been a call for more police involvement. As mentioned earlier, police involvement alone will make little or no difference in school violence. There must be an ecological approach taken to this problem. What we are looking at is something that may be in the fabric of American society where issues are moving from the bottom up rather than the top down in the culture. An analogy to this might be the evolution of jazz in which the early jazz musicians and their use of drugs were initially associated with people of color and areas such as Harlem. Had it been that we had made interventions when this violence was in other communities rather than in white middle class ones maybe this would not be happening today.

We ask why their parents did not see what was going on. Counselors and smaller class sizes may have seen this. Metal detectors would not have caught this. I reiterate it is not a question of whether the school will be a parent or not, but will it be a good parent?

Finally, human services looks at the person as a total being.[1] Ethically, the human service worker must take what the client says at face value. Oftentimes, however, the problem that the client presents is not the real problem. The real problem will be ferreted out by the helper who is an active listener. Also, it must be kept in mind that clients rarely have one problem; they have multiple problems with multiple causes. Multiple problems with multiple causes call for sophisticated responses.

CONCLUSION

I close this chapter with some musings about 1999 two Larry King shows that I watched the week of April 26 in which he had such notable child experts as T. Barry Brazelton, Joseph Garbarino, and Stanton Saminow on. Listening to these men, it was clear that we must be con-

---

[1]These five concepts are more fully discussed in Naomi Brill, *Working With People.*

crete and specific when making suggestions to people who are working at the level of the family, the school, and the community. Brazelton talked about self-image and the motivation to learn and that we need to see that these are taught to our young children. He also pointed out that when a new baby is born that if the mothers voice is heard and the baby turns not toward her but toward someone else that this is truly an early early sign that interventions are called for. Garbarino and Saminow talked about self-image. This is certainly a beginning, but not enough.

Brazelton went on to say that the values of American culture of war, money, and aggression can only lead to the kinds of behaviors that we are seeing. This ties in nicely with my points on culture and that we need to look at the culture and the structure of the culture rather than look at individual deviation. Brazelton also pointed out that firearm deaths in America today are twelve times higher than the next twenty-five countries combined.

In conclusion, I say that we must have specific answers, for those who want to take the theory of human services and make it work in today's turbulent world. These include being better listeners and problem solvers. By being active listeners we will not be mislead by what children and families are saying. We may also respond more often with appropriate interventions by being active listeners. Focusing on problems in living such as alcohol and drugs, self-concept, mental illness, and abuse both mental and physical, we should be able to prevent some of these behaviors before they escalate into horrific behaviors in the future. We must focus on both curricular as well as non-curricular issues that students and families have and that students bring to the school.

By focusing on the school as a one-stop shopping center we can begin to handle the problems that are so real in our society today and ones that are being aimed in the direction of our schools. The school may be the focus of frustration for students today. Hence, it *can be* a seamless organization where these problems are handled by human service workers who are a part of the school community.

Throughout all of this there is a need for coordination of services. By having singular focal points for interventions such as schools, coordination should be accomplished at least to a more significant degree than at present. I close with an analogy from my youth in the 1950s growing up in Florida. At that point in time my mother believed drinking cold water after getting overheated caused polio, (she was not the only mother who believed this). Not long after this many public swimming pools were closed, because it was believed that they were another source of polio.

• Polio scare closes pools!
• School violence (perceptual or real) closes schools!

We need to be aware of hysteria and quick fixes. In the human services, there are no quick fixes. Hysteria may continue as we approach high school graduations across the country. A coordinated effort involving education, human services, mental health, and law enforcement may hopefully lead to long-term genuine change that is needed in and by American society. Reliance on quick fixes may partially explain the state of affairs of America's children and families today.

Chapter 2

FULL SERVICE SCHOOLS: THE ULTIMATE IN HUMAN SERVICE DELIVERY

INTRODUCTION

ONE IN FOUR CHILDREN GROWING UP IN AMERICA cannot become a healthy self-sustaining adult without immediate attention. The primary institutions that traditionally carry the responsibility for raising and teaching children - families and schools - cannot fulfill these obligations without immediate and intensive assistance (Dryfoos, 1994, p. 205).

Joy Dryfoos (1994) entitles her book *Full Service Schools: A revolution in health and services for children, youth and families.* Truly it is a revolution, but how sad that it is a revolution. We should be so far beyond what she draws up in this book. Yet we are woefully behind in instituting wraparound services for children. We are woefully behind in seeing that children come to school well-fed, well-clothed, and safe from harm. We have tended to ignore the non-curricular reasons that put students at risk. The full service school is a direct onslaught to deal with the atrocities that are perpetrated on young people K through 12 as they enter the school system in America today.

Dryfoos's proposal is one that learns from other research particularly Project A.L.A.S. Rumberger & Larson (1994), that illustrates that add-on programs to existing schools are doomed to fail. We seem to be so happy with tinkering with

12

and fixing the school but not with making needed thorough-
going changes. The full service school is, in fact, this change.
It is the beginning, if you will, of linkages between human
services and school personnel.

It goes without saying that many of our preschool children
come to school curricularly non-prepared. In Tennessee,
one in five children comes to school for kindergarten not
knowing their primary colors. If they don't know primary
colors, we can only imagine what else it is that they don't
know. Hence, these kids are truly at risk. It would appear
that both curricular and non-curricular causes of failure are
inextricably linked. Charles Hargis (1990) points out that
children enter first grade at reading levels of about 1.5 years
in variation. He notes that as children progress through
school the range of this reading variation increases. Hence
you have both curricular and non-curricular reasons for early
at-risk status.

The full service school by working to meet the ecological
and total needs of the child begins prevention and intervention at an early age and seeks to see that inequities between
the haves and have-nots are diminished. The full service
school certainly does not punish the haves of society. In fact,
they can only benefit from a system such as this. As an
example, if my child is well, the possibilities of your child
being well are only increased. Children who come to school
sick can only make the other children sick. There will come
a point in time when urban removal and white flight can no
longer occur. There just will not be any place else to go. In
other words, there is going to come a time when the middle
class or the haves, to use a term from Saul Alinsky, will have
to come to grips with the realities of American society in the
late twentieth century and begin to deal with the problems
that only a full service school can attend to.

In describing what she means by full service schools,
Dryfoos (1994) says:

I have described a new way of looking at the school as a piece of real estate that we all own, where our most precious future assets are trained to become responsible adults, schools which could be so vastly enriched by the addition of a whole array of community resources. (p. xvii)

They (full service schools) are located in buildings especially designed to incorporate the concept of integrated services. They are facilities that can offer a seamless experience for the students, parents, and staff. School, community, and agency personnel have common and shared goals and participate in joint decision making. The movement toward full service schools must encompass both quality education and support services. (Dryfoos, 1994, p. 143)

Full service schools provide the most comprehensive set of services and are technically defined as "integrated education, medical, social, and/or human services" provided in school facilities in locations easily accessible to them. Among the services provided are public benefits such as Aid to Families with Dependent Children (AFDC*), parenting skills, counseling for abused children, and adult education (Dryfoos, 1994, p. 230). "Much of the rhetoric supporting comprehensive care for children and youth, links the goals of school success with the desire toward changes in health behaviors" (Dryfoos, 1994, p. 164).

As mentioned earlier, add-on programs are not going to be successful. Programs must be started from scratch so to speak. Hence, I think what Dryfoos (1994) is saying is that we have this addition of services but we also have a change in philosophy as to what it is that the school is all about. It is more than simply add-ons. As she says, "A school based approach requires that schools connect strongly with the health and social service systems" (p. xi).

---

* Under new federal and state guidelines AFDC is not provided though some form of financial aid may be.

Today's schools feel pressured to feed children; provide psychological support services; offer health screening; establish networks relating to substance abuse, child welfare, and sexual abuse; cooperate with the local police and probation officers; add curriculum for prevention of substance abuse, teen pregnancy, suicide, and violence (the morbidities); and actively promote social skills, good nutrition, safety, and general health. (Dryfoos, 1994, p. 5)

As Fuller (1996) states in his article *Revolution not reform: Only radical transformation of U. S. education will save the neediest children*, we must also fight for policies in this country that will liberate millions of poor and minority children from the appalling conditions that suck the promise out of their lives (p. 4).

Dryfoos states that "It is her belief that one in four children, age 10 to 17, in the United States do it all" (p. 3). By this she means they use drugs, have unprotected intercourse, or are truant and fall behind in school. As a result, these seven million young people will never be able to make it without massive changes in their current circumstances. Kronick (1997) has stated, "That it is no longer a question as to whether the school will be a parent or not, it is will it be a good parent" (p. 15). Dryfoos refers to the school as a surrogate parent.

On January 19, 1997, radio station WIVK A.M. 990, in Knoxville, Tennessee, reported that Tennessee ranked number one in the nation in the prescription of Ritalin. The reader of the news commented that the state's top medical officers were going to begin looking into this immediately and that it might be assumed that the children were being bored to death in daycare and in their schools; and, hence, were reacting to this situation. The school's reaction to the children was to provide Ritalin. How interesting it is that author after author, too many to mention, have pointed out that at-risk youth are more a result of the school system than of any individual qualities which they may have. (See Kronick, 1997; Rossi, 1994; and Kronick & Hargis, 1990).

Kronick and Hargis (1990) list several factors that put individuals at risk, but still make the point that it is the school which pushes children out and which needs to be looked at far more than the individual conditions which the child has. In fact, many authors are now beginning to use the term "from risk to resilience." Higgs and Tarsi (1997) have even gone so far as to say "That at risk youth may be the saviors of the school system" (p.130). This is because the at-risk child points out the many shortfalls and the need for so many programs in regular schools. Much research in the area of alternative schools cites that it is the personal relationship that occurs between the teacher and the student that tends to make for the success of the student within the alternative school. This relationship is not reported to exist in their regular school (Kronick and Hargis, 1990).

Dryfoos notes "That a universal call has been issued for one stop, unfragmented, health and social service systems that are consumer-oriented, developmentally appropriate, and culturally relevant." She goes on to say "That schools can be seen as central institutions in the community to provide an important, if not critical, organizing focus for the coordination and integration of services" (Dryfoos, 1994, p. 11).

The important point is that the school is an omnipresent agency in American society and is in a very unique position to serve as a centrifugal force drawing people in and providing human services to them, along with the educational services that they have historically provided.

The Heart of the Full Service School

Dryfoos puts health care at the heart of the full service school. She obviously has read Abraham Maslow and believes that you must meet the most basic needs of the student before moving up the hierarchy of needs. Dryfoos found that students who report higher rates of high-risk behaviors, such as substance abuse and earlier initiation of sexual intercourse have been proven more likely to use school-based clinics than other students. Now the more conservative amongst us might say by going to these clinics these students are engaging in these behaviors. The key issue to be watched out for is not to create a program that leads to the high risk behavior that we are trying to prevent. However, it becomes clear that this is not the case (i.e., that students engage in these high-risk behaviors because of going to the clinic) because Dryfoos also points out that Glade Central High School in Palm Beach County, Florida, reported a drop in the pregnancy rate of 73 percent when a school-based clinic was instituted in their school. She also notes that because minor illnesses such as headaches, menstrual cramps and accidents on school property can be treated in school, absences and excuses to go home have decreased. In centers with mental health personnel, substantial numbers of students and their families are gaining access to psychosocial counseling that was not available to them within the community. Dryfoos says that the demand is overwhelming. To borrow a phrase from Kevin Costner in Field of Dreams, "if you build it, they will come."

Dryfoos further states that, "Utilization figures show that the characteristics of students who use the centers generally mirror those of the school population with slightly higher usage by females, African Americans and younger students" (Dryfoos, 1994, pp. 133-135). It appears that certain high-risk behaviors are definitely impacted by the institution of the core facet of the full service school (i.e., the health clinic). There is more to full service schools than health clinics but they are at the center and are her linchpin or beginning point. As a way of keeping pace with changes in health care within the school setting, the University of Colorado School of Nursing has initiated a program to retrain school nurses to become school nurse practitioners who can staff primary care clinics (Dryfoos, 1994, p. 48).

According to Dryfoos (1994), leaders in the nursing field believe that school nursing is in transition from band-aids to an emphasis on preventive medicine, counseling, community outreach, and teaching. This reflects an enlargement of the role of nursing and medicine in schools and communities where some of the most basic needs are not being attended to. Within this new nursing model, the school nurse is a critical link between the school and the family.

With this expansion of the nursing role, the school nurse must engage in the process of collaboration and linkages become extremely important with the school, family and community. Nurses, teachers and human service workers will have new and expanded roles under this new model. New skills will have to be taught in colleges and universities that teach collaboration as a method of interaction. In-service training will have to focus on the same skills. Agency administrators, at the same time, will have to make program linkages especially in a time of shrinking budgets.

School-Linked and School-Based Services

In determining where to put human services in relationship to education and schools, the following four issues are especially salient.

1. Should the services be located in the school, adjacent to the school, or in a separate location away from the school?
2. How to integrate and link the services so that they are more than add-ons.
3. Issues of turfism.
4. Do support services water down academic quality?

The issue regarding physical location of services has to do with how to get clients to come for service. One argument has it that families will not come for services if they are located in the school because they have had bad experiences in the school. The counter argument to this is to have the services at the school so that individuals and families have a good feeling about the school because of the services they have received. Research by Kronick and Stinnett (1997) on Family Resource Centers found families to be willing to come for service when these services were located within the school. If a separate entrance was provided this was all to the good.

There are many reasons why people do not come for human service. Kronick and Hargis (1990) list several barriers to coming for human service. They focus on accessability, presumed competence of the providers, awareness of the severity of the problem, and stigma.

Focusing on school-based services where the services are on site at the school, the issue of accessability is all but eliminated. Even if all interactions at the school have not been positive, most parents will tend to see their children's teachers as somewhat competent. By having the services' site-based, a halo effect may well spill over to the human service providers. Of course, a negative halo effect is also possible in this situation. It is the opinion of this author that co-location of services will enhance the competence of both teachers and human service providers.

Parents often underestimate the severity of their children's school-based problems. They often think that the problem will go away or that school officials are exaggerating the problem. Denial is a major road block for school and human service providers to overcome. By working together, teachers and human service workers can help persons take that crucial first step in asking for help.

Stigma is attached to help-seeking behavior. That should not ever be the case but it is. Asking for help says that I cannot do it myself. *Resistance* thus becomes a force to be reckoned with by the educator and the human service provider. Stigma is a socially created category and education regarding this issue must be addressed not only to the people being served but to society at large.

School-linked services are going to be perceived as add-on services. Add-on services have been shown to be unequivocally ineffective. Also by being in a different location from the school, these services may be geographically and/or physically inaccessible. The separate site may be stigmatizing as well as inaccessible. School sites at their worst are neutral places for families to be seen.

In essence, school-based services are seen as superior to school-linked services. Since the stated purpose of school-based programs is to give the students and their families maximum access to the services they need, where they are, it seems more efficient to integrate the services into the school environment to achieve the seamless effect (Dryfoos, 1994, p. 143). Yet it is crystal clear that school-based centers will never be so comprehensive that they obviate the need for all referrals, so in that sense, all programs will require linkages to different community agencies.

Fallout from Full Service Schools–Changes!

Some teachers who have been in the system for a long time feel that the school should not be the place for the provision of services and that these outsiders only intrude on the smooth running of the institution (Dryfoos, 1994, p. 152).

Compare the above statement with the next two. In response to the growing interest in integrated youth programing, consideration is being given to a new category of personnel–someone with cross-disciplinary training who can manage and coordinate multi-competent, multi-agency programs (Dryfoos, 1994, p. 163).

A program change that should serve as a harbinger for all educators comes from Miami University of Ohio. The University has called for the creation of human service professionals, who are trained to focus on children's needs across disciplines (Dryfoos, 1994).

State universities should be encouraged to produce new kinds of comprehensive youth service workers and teachers with cross-disciplinary approaches involving schools of education, psychology, public health, medicine, nursing and social work (Dryfoos, 1994).

It is clear that colleges and universities must undergo changes in order to educate and train the new human service professionals of the twenty-first century. The processes involved here are multidisciplinary, intercollegiate, flexibility and humanistic. The human service worker and the new teacher must be able to communicate with each other with no concerns for turfism.

A direct follow-through from this type of logic is the report of one program manager and it is especially inciteful. This manager found that, rather than necessarily having education credentials in a specific field, staff had to be flexible, culturally sensitive, creative, highly organized, very dedicated, willing to work hard, tolerate stress, and genuinely care about people (Dryfoos, 1994). This line of reasoning is in concert with what has been suggested in the counseling field. Researchers such as Eysenck (1952) have reported that the counselor is more important than the counseling technique. Combs and Snygg (1959) reported many of the same personal qualities as the manager above as being important for the counselor. In the final analysis, the need is for new professionals, new organizations, and new ways of doing things in colleges and universities as well as the field. The time for all of this is now!

Chapter 3

HUMAN SERVICE–SCHOOL COLLABORATION

INTRODUCTION

ONE IN FOUR CHILDREN IN AMERICA CANNOT BECOME A HEALTHY, self-sustaining adult without immediate attention. Families and schools cannot fulfill their obligations without immediate and intensive assistance.

In one-fifth of America's eighty thousand schools, one-half of the children are eligible for subsidized meals, (Dryfoos, 1994).

In *Dealing With Dropouts* (Kronick & Hargis, 1998) we found that the Lock-Step Curriculum, the Healthy, Out of Jail, and Employed Curriculum (H.O.J.E.), and prevention and early intervention are key processes to examine. These terms, along with collaboration, constitute the central facet of working with children within a one-stop shopping approach. Children are coming into the human services system at an earlier age and with more disturbing behaviors than ever before. Our correctional schools are filled. Juvenile courts see a crime rate growing faster than the adult rate. Many of these courts are so inundated with delinquent offenses such as murder, arson, rape, or assault that they will no longer hear status offender cases such as truancy or unruly behavior. It has been my experience that the correctional system is full; that it transfers many of its cases to mental health, oftentimes for nothing more than thirty-day evaluations, and that the children who were formerly treated in mental health facilities are now being cared for and treated in our public schools.

As a system, the child care management program is in disarray. Not only do we have too many children being handled through a court of record, the juvenile court, but also we have too many children in foster care, who are eligible for adoption but are lost in a bureaucratic maze. This is a result of fragmentation of services.

Full Service Schools

A full service school where there is collaboration between human services and school personnel will help bring an end to these types of human service delivery system problems.

> The time has come for a new conception of the responsibilities of the school. The lives of youth are desperate, parents bring up their children in surroundings which make them in large numbers vicious and criminally dangerous. Some agency must take charge of the entire problem of child life and master it. (Robert Hunter, 1904, Social Reformer)

> The school should serve as a clearing house for children's activity so that all child welfare agencies may be working simultaneously and efficiently, thus creating a child's world within the city wherein all children may have a wholesome environment all of the day and every day. (William Wort, Superintendent of Schools, Gary, Indiana, 1923)

> All agencies dealing with neglected or behavior problem children should be closely coordinated under the aegis of the school including medical inspection, school nursing, attendance control, vocational guidance and placement, psychological testing, visiting teachers, and special schools and classes. (Thomas D. Elliott, 1928, Sociologist, and Calfee et. al., 1998, p. 7)

According to Tyack (1992), there is a long history in the United States of providing remediation services to children in a school setting. Early programs attempted to provide health and social services in the school setting. The intent of these early efforts was to assist immigrant children in adjusting to their new culture. Locating these services in the school changed the focus from serving the family to serving the individual child (Lawson and Anderson 1996).

This shift in focus followed a dichotomus model of services discussed by Parlin and Grew (1996) as nationalism and developmentalism. The intent of each doctrine was the preservation of a revolutionary government in the early eighteenth century. The concept of using education to preserve and protect the nation from external attacks as well as internal disintegration, developing national wealth and economic independence and a national unity through common goals, ideals, and traditions expressed in a state directed national curriculum was the theory of nationalism (Parlin & Grew, 1996, p. 151).

The developmental theory of education views the child as the object of the educational process, not the country's continuance. These theorists believed that education could change society for the better by changing individuals who made up the society. They focused on the nature of the mind and how psychologically the mind worked, with support for their theory evolving from the study of the development of children (Parlin & Grew, 1996, p. 151).

As the 1800s moved along, industrialization buttressed by the creation and introduction of machinery led to specialization in trades, increases in family wealth, growth in population and increases in immigration and the concentration of people in cities (Parlin & Grew, 1996).

These developments had shocking affects on the family. The home was no longer self-sufficient. These societal changes led to changes in public education. There became increasingly intensive demands that all children be educated at public expense for a definite period of time each year and for a definite period of years. These demands led to the first compulsory attendance laws in Massachusetts which were enacted in 1852 (Parlin & Grew, 1996, p. 152).

From this historical evolution came the development of child labor laws in America. The children of this period often disclosed family economic difficulties as the reason for their need to work. Working from the developmental model, discussed above, where the individual's importance was key led to the development of social services in the form of food, clothing, and basic medical services for poor indigent children. These services grew out of what was learned from talking with and listening to the children (qualitative research) and the evolution of compulsory public education. This approach used Maslow's theory 80 years before he developed it.

In 1913 Helen Todd, a factory inspector in Chicago, systematically questioned 500 children of immigrants about working and going to school: Would they choose to continue working long hours in the sweat shops, or would they choose to go to school if they did not have to work? Four hundred and twelve children told her that they preferred factory labor to the monotony, humiliation, and even sheer cruelty that they experienced in school. This book is an attempt to put an end to that line of thinking and to promote the concept of the school as a human service agency. We believe that it is no longer a question of whether the school will be a parent or not; the question is whether it will be a good parent.

The school as a human service agency can go a long way toward reducing our criminal and psychiatric populations, our welfare rolls, and our indigents in need of medical care.

All of us who participated in this book are committed not only to the acquisition of knowledge by students, but also to the prevention and remediation of problems for all those at-risk students whom we have yet to serve.

Obviously these problems are timeless. People have been speaking of full service schools for almost a century. At the same time, changing times demand changing approaches in delivering human services.

The full service school of today co-locates services as well as collaborates with human services that are in the community. Collaboration and from the ground up decision making are key facets of the full service school. The full service school is a community hub for services to children and families. It provides services that the community defines as needed. These may range from providing a laundromat to delivering adult education. Providing health care is a central tenet of full service schools. A child who is hungry, abused, using drugs and or alcohol cannot learn. The most basic needs of the child and family must be addressed. Once the needs are defined, interventions will be designed and put into practice. Barriers to service, including resistance and reluctance, will be studied so as to prepare the action plan and the successful delivery of service.

A driving caveat is that "the concept of full service schools where schools and communities work together in coordinated delivery of services to children and families is ready for realization." The academic and social services need of children cannot be separated from the needs of the family unit. Nor can delivery of these services be neatly separated according to agency. Whether we like it or not, we as a society are very inter dependent (Calfee et al., 1998, p. XI).

Labeling, segregating, counting, and treating the family's complex problems has served only to create a system that funds countless agencies; duplicates services, functions inefficiently, and fails to improve the educational, social, medical, and financial lives of the people it is meant to serve (Calfee, 1998, p. 1).

The most important institution for children whose families

are not able to provide the support they need is the school!

A full service school means a school which serves as a central point of delivery, a central community hub for whatever education, health, social and human and/or employment services, have been determined locally to be needed to support a child's success in school and in the community (Calfee, et al., 1998, p.7).

All agencies dealing with neglected or behavior problem children should be closely coordinated under the aegis of schools including medical inspection, school nursing, attendance control, vocational guidance and placement, psychological testing, visiting teachers in special schools and classes. (Calfee, et al., 1998, p. 7).

Because children bring these problems into the school setting, growing numbers of children are less ready to learn and academic success is severely affected. The existing system has failed because of the following five points:

1. Most services are crisis-oriented.
2. The existing welfare system divides problems into rigid categories.
3. The lack of coordination and collaboration
4. Specialized agencies are unable to meet the needs of families with multiple problems.
5. A lack of adequate funding.

Services that can be offered through full service schools include:

• Adult education
• Case work
• Child care
• Community use of school activities
• Economic services
• Health services
• Juvenile alternative services
• Latch-key services
• Mental health counseling

• Pre-kindergarten services.

This model will, in a sense, refocus the school. The following are six steps that should aid in planning the full service school.

1. Identify the problem–do a needs assessment–gather data
2. Identify services that the families need and want
3. Identify duplication and gaps in services
4. Identify a target group
5. Identify barriers to service delivery
6. Develop an action plan. This may be the most important part.

It is not enough to point out what is lacking. The full service school must deliver necessary services.

The patchwork of funding strategies now used for school linked services has resulted in small scale, temporary programs, rather than long term programs that are systematically developed and funded. A full service model creates a single common eligibility assessment for use by all agencies. A full service model presents the opportunity to establish inter-agency collaboration thus paving the way for cost sharing and reducing duplication. There needs to be data on the impact of services. Process and outcome evaluation need to be built in from the very beginning.

Strategies

• Provide services that have the most value
• Early intervention and prevention at a young age
• Collaboration
• Plan *with* families not *for* them
• Flexible funding–multiple sources–local, state, federal, private
• Governing structures should be collaborative
• Use existing funds as much as possible

- Place a high value on families
- Focus on achieving and documenting desired results—the importance of assessment—process and outcome evaluation—these are important parts of inter-agency collaboration
- Build in approaches to service delivery that continue regardless of community changes
- Develop and expand programs through communication and training

We cannot fix schools without paying attention to the students, their families, and their communities. The most recognizable symptom of high-risk status is school failure. Schools are increasingly being called on to be surrogate parents.

A universal call has been issued for one-stop, un-fragmented health and social service systems that are consumer-oriented, developmentally appropriate, and culturally relevant. The school is an organizer of community services. The school nurse is a critical link between the school and the family.

Full service schools are located in buildings especially designed to incorporate the concept of integrated services—facilities that can offer a seamless experience for students, parents, and staff. School and community agency personnel have common and shared goals and participate in joint decision making in a full service school.

The human service education professional is one who can work in the school.

The staff need to be:
- Flexible
- Culturally sensitive
- Creative
- Highly organized, very dedicated, willing to work hard and tolerate stress, and generally care about people.

State universities should be encouraged to produce new

kinds of comprehensive youth service workers and teachers with cross-disciplinary approaches involving schools of education, psychology, public health, medicine, nursing, social work, and human services. A thorough understanding of collaboration is required here.

The concept of collaboration is a key facet of full service schools. It is characterized by the following seven components.

1. Communication
2. Clear agreements
3. Decision making
4. Monitoring and evaluation
5. Recognition
6. Trust
7. Leadership

(Lawson & Anderson, 1996, p. 162)

James Comer

The school is the most natural place to help children for there is no stigma attached. (Comer, 1990)

The most important institution for children whose families are not able to provide the support they need is the school. (Beyond Rhetoric, 1991, p 210)

Due to the fact that families have undergone a major societal change, it is even more important for schools and communities to take part in family care.

These three statements grow out of the voluminous work of James Comer, Professor of Child Psychiatry at Yale. Comer's social development model operates on the belief that academic success is dependent upon the school's ability to meet the social and mental health needs of children, as well as their families. Central to this model is the school management and governance team which includes school personnel, parents, and members of the school community.

Comer's schools are largely in inner-city poor neighborhoods. One has only to visit New Haven to see how tough these neighborhoods are. Comer did not select "easy pickings." There are approximately 750 Comer schools in America today.

James Comer is a name that all human service providers should be familiar with, but probably aren't. Comer, though trained as a physician, was affected by the Chicago School of Sociology. I am intrigued by this because I, too, see a strong contribution from the Chicago School to human service theory. Comer's schools are influenced by Robert Park and Ernest Burgess. I will give a brief outline of the contributions from the Chicago School that apply in Comer's schools and add a few of my favorites. I believe the model is quite robust in trying to understand children and their involvement in schools and human services.

Comer understood that all of us go to school. He also saw the school as a place to deliver human services because of its lack of stigma. From Ernest Burgess (1927), he learned about the importance of place. Burgess developed what he termed the concentric zone theory of behavior. Simply put, Burgess posited that as groups moved away from the central city, disorganized behavior decreased. Burgess saw the central city as a place of disorganization and social deviance. His work, along with the later work of Faris and Dunham (1966), posited that regardless of what groups live in these zones, behaviors would remain the same in that zone.

Comer's work utilized this information and provided useful tools for the creation of Cozi (Comer Ziegler) Schools utilizing human service workers in the schools.

Robert Park (1967) also had a strong influence on Comer. From Park, Comer learned the importance of listening to people in their natural environment. Park was influential in having Chicago students learn while they were in the field. This was also the progenitor for one school of thought in qualitative research.

Symbolic interaction is a theory that evolved directly from the Chicago School. The following four questions are heuristic for those working with children and families in a school setting.

1. How do people define themselves, others, and their settings, and their activities?
2. How do people's definitions and perspectives develop and change?
3. What is the fit between different perspectives held by different people?
4. What is the fit between people's perspectives and their activities? (Taylor and Bogdan, 1984, p. 136)

Comer develops four policies that evolve from his theoretical model.

1. The need for preschool readiness programs.
2. The interface of school programs and human services.
3. School management that is top down must become collaborative.
4. The family must be involved in a meaningful way in the workings of the school. (Comer, 1996, p. 23)

Comer emphatically states, "difficult social interactions between students and schools compound skill and knowledge development and lead to early school failure." (Comer, 1996, p. 7) Early school failure leads to behavior problems and dropping out.

This set of assumptions is a natural place for school personnel and human service providers to collaborate. Human service workers are especially educated and trained to work with children of all ages in this type of situation.

Children who don't do well in school educationally and/or behaviorally often get in trouble at home for this behavior. This merely compounds the problem. It is better to deal with school problems at school and family problems at home. Punishing the child at home for school problem behavior exacerbates the problem and may lead to violence escalation. This violent behavior may surface at school, home, or in the community. This scenario provides the opportunity for human service providers to work in schools and to do prevention. Comer's findings provide exciting opportunities for school personnel and human service workers to make a real difference in children and families lives.

Comer posits four outcomes from parental involvement in schools:

1. Teachers learn more about their students.
2. Parents become more motivated to learn.
3. Schools sustain educational change.
4. With family school collaboration, the school becomes a prominent force in the community.

All of these are vital opportunities for human services and schools to work together in a collaborative process. Kurt Lewin, (1951) is another influence on Comer. Lewin's field theory which states that behavior is driven by the interactions of the individual with the environment is congruent with the work of Burgess described above. Lewin stresses the importance of how the field is defined by the individual. What was important was perception of the field not the field itself. This is tied strongly to another member of the Chicago School, W.I. Thomas (1967). Thomas posited what he termed the definition of the situation. Simply put, Thomas stated, "If you define a situation as real, it is real in its consequences." This is all a good theoretical base for human services. It is especially well suited for school human service collaborative work.

Human Development

The stress on human development is a central tenet of Comer's approach. Comer urges that education must be developmentally appropriate for the child. He argues that education that is presented to the child must take into account the developmental stage of the child.

Erickson's (1963) developmental model contains the following seven stages. These stages are both heuristic and functional. To any human service worker or teacher knowledge of this model is critical.

- Stage one, zero to one year, trust vs. mistrust
- Stage two, one to three years, autonomy vs. doubt
- Stage three, four to five years, initiative vs. guilt
- Stage four, six to twelve years, industry vs. inferiority
- Stage five, thirteen to seventeen years, identity vs. role confusion
- Stage six, eighteen to thirty-five years, intimacy vs. isolation
- Stage seven, thirty-six to sixty-five, generativity vs. stagnation
- Stage eight, sixty-six on, integrity vs. despair

It will be helpful to clients if human service workers broadly defined, understand and can work with clients utilizing this information. A client is helped by the human service provider saying to them, "You know, within limits, this behavior is to be expected and with time, this behavior will slowly change."

A counselor working with children between the ages of twelve and eighteen will see them pass through three stages. Human service workers integrating a developmental approach will make their counseling style much more effective. A counselor who uses reality therapy, behaviorism, person-centered counseling, or any other approach for that matter will be much more effective when counseling within a developmental perspective. Add to this, placing human services within a school and a powerful, systemic delivery of services is in place. I see this configuration as a major opportunity for collaboration in human service delivery. In the twenty-first century, school-based human services offer an opportunity to improve the delivery of services to children and their families.

Dilemmas

Two frustrating issues have long existed within human services: (1.) Human services offers services and programs that people do not need or want, and (2.) people are not motivated to use existing services or they use them for the wrong reasons, i.e., services are used for baby-sitting rather than for learning. A great many of my college students believe that clients are not motivated and don't care about their children. These are thorny issues worthy of a great deal of debate. At this point, I believe it is my job as an instructor in human services to have students think about the motivation of their clients and also to teach them ways to motivate the client so that they will in fact use the services that are so necessary. Hence, I see a genuine opportunity when human services and schools collaborate.

The Lock Step curriculum is another force that is particularly relevant regarding the drop out rate and the at risk potential for students today. This particular concept is of more import to the educator than the human service worker but information on it here is presented so that the human service worker working in this environment may well understand their role in working with those who have been defined by both Betts (1946) and Hargis (1987 & 1998) as curriculum casualties.

Betts (1946) stated that many reading problems were created simply because we do not make adjustments to deal with individual differences. Undoubtedly, some reading disabilities are caused when a child is required to start reading instruction before he/she is generally ready. Betts estimated at the time that about 15% of the children were so disabled. Later he elaborated on the problem attributing it also to the *Lock Step* nature of school organization. Here instruction was provided based on the assumption that every child was to climb the same curriculum ladder. Objectives were set up in grade levels. Each level represented a rung on the curricular ladder. At about the same chronological age, usually six, children took the first step, the first grade. The goal of each teacher was to prepare the class for the next grade. The grade itself was broken into units of work through which all children were to proceed. Reading programs and content areas alike were designed for these gradations or steps on the assumption that all children are capable of uniform achievement. Children who could not manage to maintain this rate of achievement might be provided with remedial instruction to help them achieve grade level. Those who could not keep the pace were either socially promoted or repeated a grade. The same rate of learning progress was required of all children regardless of the individual intrinsic readiness level or speed of learning. (Hargis, 1987, p. 4)

In looking at the concept of push outs or how the school pushes the student out, Kronick & Hargis (1998) make the point that the factor which contributes most to this problem is not within the dropout or potential dropout but in the schools from which they leave. More precisely, this factor is the curriculum. The curriculum defines the way that schools are organized and instruction is delivered. Curricular organization determines the way students are evaluated and the ratio of success to failure that results. When a student drops out of school, the curriculum is virtually always a factor. It can be the primary factor or a contributing factor but it is always a factor.

One may think of a curriculum as a benign list of educational objectives or skills that make up a course of study. In one sense, it may be. However, the scope and sequence of items that make up the typical K-12 curriculum make up a matrix to which students must be fitted. It is in this fitting that the damage occurs and students drop out or are forced out, hence the term push outs. Rather than being dropouts, these students are actually better characterized as casualties. Injury inflicted on students in the attempts at fitting them to rigid curricular structures makes them curriculum casualties (Kronick & Hargis, 1998, p. 11).

Two alternatives to this Lock Step notion are the H.O.J.E. curriculum, that is healthy, out of jail, and employed and curriculum-based assessment. Curriculum-based assessment is the tailoring of the curriculum to the child rather than forcing the child into the existing curriculum. This seems to be self evident and something that educators could do, that is to take individual difference into account when teaching. However, this seems to be something to which a great deal of verbiage is expended but not much is done. A more complete elaboration of this dilemma is certainly needed but is not within the scope of this chapter. The last concept is that of the H.O.J.E. curriculum, that is healthy, out of jail, and employed. For the human service worker this curriculum is one in which they would be well apprized to acquaint themselves. That is how schools can provide a curriculum for those students who are not college bound but for whom the capacity to be healthy, out of jail, and employed is a worthy goal both for the individual and for society?

CONCLUSION

The aim of this chapter has not been to showcase the problems of children in America today. This is done every day in the popular media as well as in our academic literature. This chapter does make the point, however, that when it comes to corrections, mental health, and welfare, that the needs and problems of children are enormous. The juvenile crime rate is evolving at an increasing rate. Crimes against children are not decreasing and are more heinous than our imagination would allow us to conjure up. I am professionally involved in the case of a child, now seven, who was first abused by his father when he was two. After five years, this little boy does not have a permanent home that is safe and happy. Mental health needs of children are not being met adequately either. The Individuals with Disability Education Act (IDEA) takes up so much of the school's time with special education students that precious little is left for the students who need special attention but are not labeled Attention Deficit Hyperactive Disorder (ADHD). Mental health services are especially convoluted because of third party payments and managed care. Too many children with mental health problems are being treated in schools that are not particularly well qualified to deal with these types of problems.

The fastest growing segment of the homeless population is mothers and children. Approximately one-third of homeless are children under 18.

Even with the number of people coming off welfare rolls, there are still problems with the number of children on welfare. This chapter presents a model that includes school human services collaboration, full service schools, knowledge of human development, the Comer school model, and emphasis on prevention to combat these problems.

This is where persons and their environment certainly interact!

Chapter 4

THE TENNESSEE CONSORTIUM FOR THE DEVELOPMENT OF FULL SERVICE SCHOOLS

JERRY MORTON

INTRODUCTION

THE TENNESSEE CONSORTIUM FOR THE DEVELOPMENT of Full Service Schools (TCDS) was created to promote and assist in the development of full service schools throughout Tennessee. Its creation came about as the result of area professionals' recognition that the prevalent delivery models of services to children do not adequately address all of the components in a child's environment. Those delivery systems compartmentalize specific categories of the child's experience and treat them as independent and discrete components to be fixed, adjusted or left undisturbed. The unstated assumption is that a malfunctioning part of the child's life does not significantly affect the other dimensions of the child's interactive world. For example, in a one dimensional delivery of service model, if the child is failing in reading at his school, then the school should work harder to teach him to read. If the school does this then the child will learn to read and be a better student. The fact that the child does not sleep at night due to fears about being left alone because both of his parents work night shifts has no bearing on his reading problems. In turn, the fact that the child feels depressed about his poor academic behavior towards his mother when she asks him to help with chores around the house. Similarly, the fact that the child's mother has to travel thirty minutes to the laundromat to do the week's washing rather than spend that time reading to the child has no impact on the child's reading difficulties at school. Logic and experience tell us that all of these components are interlocked, yet our intervention systems are oriented to be one-dimensional in trying to assist the child.

Every agency and school system has acknowledged, in principle, that the life of the child is an integrated system and have stated their desire to work with all other agencies to assist the child. At the state level, numerous interagency agreements exist to assist cooperation across departmental boundaries to better serve children. However, many of the behaviors of agencies and schools tend to reflect a belief system in conflict with the concepts of the child's interactive world and the frequent necessity for interagency cooperation to assist the child. This belief system is reflected through action rather than words. The facts that educators do not understand the juvenile justice system does not have a systematic way of communicating child-helpful information to the schools indicate that neither thinks what the other does has any significant effect on "their mission." The fact that human services does not keep the school system informed about finding children who are hungry for extended periods of time paired with the fact that most educators cannot determine which children show basic signs of hunger and malnutrition reflects a belief that being hungry has little effect upon learning or behavior. The list of fact that indicate agencies do not think what happens to a child in one sphere of his life affects another aspect of the child's experiences is quite long.

The point is clear. Despite our written interagency agreements, our well-educated articulations and our good intentions, our behavior does not fully match what it is we say we believe. Our behavior, not our words, ultimately tells us what we truly believe. The solution to this dilemma is clear. We must either change our beliefs or change our behavior. It has become obvious that we, as professionals, concerned citizens and taxpayers, are not assisting our children as effectively as we need to. The discrepancy between what we say we believe and what our behavior indicates we believe is too great to think otherwise.

Fortunately, the good will of our educators, human service-related professionals, parents and community members is not an issue of concern. The blocking factors that keep us from implementing our beliefs in assisting children have to do with strategies for delivering services lagging behind our evolving societal awareness of what needs to be done to assist every child. Many of the members of the Consortium work for schools and agencies that have system issues which interfere with the integration of their services with other agencies on behalf of children. A host of these issues have their source of conflict resting in the management of limited resources. For example, the school system receives funds to deliver specific services to children with disabilities that cannot be spent on children without those disabilities. In turn, the TennCare program has funds to deliver the same services to children for medical needs but not for educational purposes. If one or the other program delivers a needed service to the wrong category of needy children, that program has depleted its budget for a child that it was not to serve while violating a state or federal law. In the meantime, there are children who need these services who are not getting them because they don't fit the criteria of one of the agencies. In other cases, the appropriate agency has not been informed of the need of the child by the agency that found itself unable to serve the child. The failure to inform the other responsible agency can often be due to the limited time of agency staff to communicate or a lack of understanding of the other agency's capabilities to serve a child. Many of these breakdowns could be resolved simply by having the two agencies housed in the same building. This would make communications between the two much easier and quicker. Such a solution would fit into the conceptualization of a Full Service School.

Other blocking factors keeping agencies from working together on behalf of the child are numerous. They range from confidentiality laws prohibiting the exchange of information about a child, to confusion over who has parental authority over the child, to conflicting delivery models of service between agencies, to competition between agencies for the same grant money, etc.

Professionals employed by a specific agency have a responsibility to fulfill their job requirements within that agency. The nature of the funding pattern of the employing agency, its administrative structure, the location of its offices and a host of other factors often deter the professionals from collaborating across agency boundaries for more integrated services to children. The Consortium provides a bridge for the professionals to meet their agency's requirements while serving as a tool to address more effectively and resolve the larger societal issues that impede the health development of all of our children. The Consortium is also a toll for advocacy groups, community groups and concerned citizens to utilize on the common ground of our desire to find a better way of assisting children.

Commitment

The Tennessee Consortium for the Development of Full Service Schools (TCDS) is committed to being a tool for changing our behaviors to fit our stated belief systems for helping children. The vehicle it has chosen is the Full Service School concept. This concept places the school as the center of children's lives and thus the life of the community. It is the community that defines what its Full Service School provides, the way it provides its services and how it continually improves itself. The Full Service School is available to be utilized on a twenty-four hour basis. Its services could include having probation officers housed in the school during and after school hours, providing basic medical care during and after school to children and their families, maintaining a wing of the community mental health center at the school campus, installing a laundromat on campus for parents to use, having supervised after-school activities for children on the campus, etc. The list of possibilities is endless because it is the entire community that utilizes the Full Service School to fit its needs as they exist and will develop over time.

It is not the goal of the Consortium to define the Full Service School for the community. The goal of the Consortium is to promote the development of the Full Service School to be more responsive to the needs of the complete child in his full environment. To this end the Consortium promotes the concept of a Full Service School within its community and assists any community, agency or subgroup in implementing a component of a Full Service School.

Purpose

The Consortium's purpose is to help school systems, other agencies, professionals, community leaders, parents and citizens at large to (1) understand the need for full service schools, (2) recognize successful efforts in implementing components of the full service model, (3) provide assistance to those wishing to develop and implement additional components of the full service school model. It embraces all those who desire to join or utilize its services. Those involved with it are all volunteers. Many are professionals, supported by their agencies to find better ways for doing that which we know to do in order to assist our children to become all that they are capable of becoming.

To date, the Consortium has:

1. Developed a comprehensive resource book, *The Essentials of Starting a Full Service School,* describing many different ways Full Service School programs have been created and the issues involved in their creation. The book is available upon request.

2. Developed a resource library of articles and books relating to the Full Service School located in the UTK College of Nursing.

3. Assisted area school systems and organizations to write grants supporting Full Service School-related activities.

4. Established realistic evaluation strategies of Full Service School-related programs with area school systems.

5. Established a pool of professionals who have volunteered their skills and time to area organizations for the development of Full Service School-related activities.

6. Established a speaker's pool for presentations to various conferences, schools and community groups promoting the concepts of Full Service Schools.

7. Facilitated the housing of professionals from agencies serving children within area schools.

8. Other projects with the Consortium's involvement are being developed.

The Consortium will continue to evolve as its membership expands and opportunities present themselves for the further development of the Full Service School concept.

Chapter 5

AT-RISK YOUTH AND THE COLLEGE CURRICULUM

INTRODUCTION

W HAT DO TEACHERS NEED TO KNOW to be effective in the twenty-first century? Obviously they need to know their subject matter and how to teach it. Knowledge of math is a prerequisite to being a math teacher. The knowledge of how to teach math is also of critical importance. In teaching there must also be an opportunity to put knowledge into practice. It's not enough just to know. Many aspiring teachers know material but may not be able to put it into play. Hence, the need for internship learning. Many universities have gone to a five-year program where majors are attained in the college of liberal arts i.e., math, and the student spends a year to a year and a half in a college of education learning methods of teaching. I am especially concerned that these methods are too narrow both in philosophy and practice as we enter the twenty-first century.

In attempting to broaden these methods, we might want to take a look at reasons for having schools and educating children. Three reasons that are historically given are: (1) to enrich the individual student, (2) to enrich the economy (the buzz word today is human or social capital), and (3) to enrich the society, to create an educated person so necessary in a democracy.

45

I think teachers of all disciplines would benefit a great deal if they thought about what their goals are in teaching 100 students a year in third grade. The answer to this question could be couched within the three broad parameters discussed above. The answer to this question is quite different from, "Why do you want to teach," which too often is answered with I like people. Along with the discipline that one wants to teach and three societal reasons to having schools and teachers, is a third component of teacher training and preparation and that is who is being taught. What do we know about people ages 4-18? How do we convey this information to aspiring teachers? Is this material being conveyed to those who want to be teachers? Terry Vatter of the At Risk Programs Network in Ithaca, New York, and editor of the *Alternative Network Journal,* in a cogent letter to me stated:

> I read your contributions to At Risk Youth: Theory Practice Reform and was interested in your argument on changing the curriculum for aspiring teachers to include attention to at risk youth and conflict resolution. I certainly agree with you and have been keenly aware that I encountered nothing at all in my teacher training specifically designed for working with at risk youth.

I don't know how long ago she was in a teacher training program but my personal and professional knowledge tells me she is right up-to-date in November, 1999.

I am blessed to be able to teach a special education class on at-risk youth during the summer semester at the University of Tennessee, Knoxville. The average enrollment in this graduate class is 25 students. In the summer of 1999, five "regular ed" students took this course. This was up from two the prior summer. This is not a required course. So we don't require a class on at-risk youth at the University of Tennessee, Knoxville.

The Course On At-Risk Youth

I hope the reader will not think me as having the ultimate in "chutzpah" in telling you some of what I teach in this course and why I think all teachers should know something about at-risk youth and how to teach with and/or help them.

Defining who is at risk is not as simple as it might seem as measurement is a political football that rarely yields agreement.

Historically, the term *at risk* referred to the deaf and blind. Today it refers to those that are going to leave school without a diploma. When this happens what are the results? Crime, mental health, and welfare rates, are effected when students drop out of school early.

Most of the convicts I know are not high school graduates. In a study of 200 inmates done at a Tennessee prison, we found the average last grade attended was eighth and reading level was fourth grade. None of these inmates would be defined as learning disabled as they were working to the capacity that they were capable. Of the 200 inmates studied, 2 had graduated from high school the other 198 had not. Their modal offense was breaking and entering, being a thief. My guess is that this generalizes to state prisons across the country. Incarceration as an adult is a costly enterprise. Is it possible that money put into prevention during the early years, zero to five, might prevent some of these adult incarcerations? I think it's important for teachers to know and understand the juvenile justice system. They may have students who are in state custody, live in a group home, or have a probation or parole officer.

Figure 1.

Arrest	Trial/Court	Institutionalization	After Care
Caught in the Act	judge-no jury a court of	Level of Security	Return to the Community
Petition-Delinquent or	record or a human		
Status Offense	service agency?	Length of Sentence,	Individualized
		Recidivism, Chapter	Educational Plan to
	In RE: GAULT	One, and Special	Return School
School, family, or community	determinant or	Education	
	indeterminant sentence		How long until adult prison?
	Innocence, Probation, State Custody		

This is not a course in juvenile delinquency, nevertheless I believe knowledge of this system will help teachers especially if they have "correction kids" in their classes. Figure 1 describes the system in a nutshell format. I will highlight aspects that are especially relevant for teachers.

The first thing a teacher should know is the difference between a delinquent and a status offense. A delinquent is a person who commits an act that is a crime regardless of the age of the person i.e., murder, rape, arson, or assault. The status offense is a crime that only a child may commit such as truancy.

Juvenile authorities file petitions against children. The filer may be the family, school, or police. Schools and teachers must be cognizant of the fact that juvenile courts are so busy with delinquent offenses that they do not want to hear from schools that Johnny was not in school today. The court generally wants the schools to handle their truancy problems.

An empathic teacher would want to know that the United States Supreme Court guarantees juveniles the right to due process in the 1967 Arizona case known as In Re Gault. Since the juvenile court is a court of record its decisions may be overturned by a higher court based on the guidelines provided in Gault.

Sentencing may be specified times set by the court or based on meeting program goals set by the institution. I have found that by the time the youngster is placed in state custody too many have a zigzag career in crime throughout most of their adolescence. The most insidious variables here are drugs and gangs. Even in the smaller towns across America gangs are gaining a foothold. In the Tennessee institutions I have been in, gang life is alive and well. Many of these young people receive letters from adult inmates telling them they will have a place when they arrive in prison if only they will kill or hurt someone. Most of the kids know enough people in prison that a scared straight program does not have a retarding effect on them.

The kids tell me that selling drugs is too good a deal to want to stay in school. They can make far more money selling drugs than they can in legitimate work. Almost all of the kids will come to the community if only for a short while on after-care (parole). If they are successful here they may attend school within the community.

Mental health–There are many students in school today in need of mental health services. These are students who are not ADHD but rather students who are

emotionally disturbed. I am concerned that school counselors are too busy to attend to these students. These are
the students that will perpetrate school violence.

I found the following scenario to be true: corrections is
full. Corrections transfers many of its kids to mental health.
The children who should be under mental health are in the
schools. Students whose behavior got them a mental health
placement in 1970 are in public schools in 1999. The system
is backed up and many severe at-risk students are in school.
I am not sure that the community agencies are able to care
for these children.

It is imperative that teachers know as much as possible
about human service agencies. The best of all possible
worlds here is the full service school.[1] Juvenile Court
Committal Orders (JCCO) require the mental health system
to determine whether or not a child is in need of mental
health services. The system is generally given thirty days to
make this decision. This process also takes away mental
health "beds" from those who might need them for more
long-term care. Teachers need to know if their students are
receiving mental health treatment and whether they are taking the myriad of drugs being prescribed to our children
today. What these drugs are and how they effect students is
of critical importance. These drugs fall into one of the following four categories: (1) antipsychotic, (2)antidepressant,
(3) antianxiety, and (4) mood stabilizers. The most abused of
these drugs of course is ritalin. Teachers and human service
workers must have at least some knowledge of these drugs
and their effects on children and the child's ability to learn
and behave appropriately in school.[2]

Finally, the most obvious system affected by at-risk youth
is welfare. At risk who eventually drop out of school will cost
our society an incredible amount of money. First, because
they are so likely to need services and secondly, because
they tend to be underemployed or unemployed. These peo-

ple are not good employees or good consumers. Hence, they are costly to the society, the economy, and to themselves. The business community hence becomes interested in at-risk youth. This is an important focal point for schools and teachers to contend with.

Poverty is both a cause and effect of being at risk in early school leaving. It behooves us to keep children in school and to have a curriculum that is meaningful for all students. A curriculum that is tailored to the child where there are no curriculum casualties is a good place to begin.

Curricular and Non-Curricular Causes of Being At Risk

Students drop out of learning and eventually out of school because of curricular and non-curricular reasons. I am going to only briefly discuss these curricular reasons. The curriculum that is lockstep guarantees that there must be some failures. The argument is clear that tailoring the curriculum to the child and individualizing instruction is the way to reduce curriculum casualties.[3]

There are correlates of dropping out that associate with the students and the school. These will only be briefly listed and discussed here.[4] Those variables that are especially significant will be discussed presently. As far as the individual is concerned the following variables are associated with being at risk and leaving school early: race and ethnicity, geographical region, gender, IQ, socioeconomic status, and participation in school activities.

Non-whites especially American Indians, Hispanics, and blacks tend to drop out more often than their white counterparts. Migrants and seasonal farm workers have an extremely high dropout rate. By the year 2010, the non-white child will be the statistically dominant child in our public schools. Knowledge of these groups cultures is critical. These groups along with Appalachian whites tend to use one language at school and a different one at home. Appalachians often say that their home language is much more fun than their school language. The issue of language and at-risk status is a thorny intellectual issue as well as another political conundrum. I can only say that if one's primary language is Spanish they must learn to read in Spanish before they will be able to read in English.

Boys drop out more than girls. Boys drop out to work. Girls drop out because they are pregnant. I have found that schools who accommodate young mothers by providing day-care and other services will keep these young women in school. Politics and morality tend to dominate this issue quite often. Day-care centers and schools are often said to promote promiscuity. The absurdity of this is, of course, evident!

Poverty is growing fastest among America's young people. Low income students leave school earlier and more often than higher income students. The same is true for IQ. High IQ students tend to stay in school at a greater rate than low IQ students.

As the top football teams in America are in the south, the same may be said about dropouts. No correlation, of course, is intended here. Of the top ten states in dropout rates, seven are from the south. Baton Rouge, Louisiana has been at the top of the dropout list for at least the last decade.

Participation in school activities keeps students in school. At-risk youth do not play football. Teachers and schools must find alternative activities that will appeal to these students. A frisbee team comes to mind. I had success coaching volleyball at an alternative high school in the 1980s. For those of you who saw the film *October Sky*, a rocket club is not a bad idea.

Over the years one response has held up for students leaving school early. "School was not for me!"

The School as a Human Service Agency

Students do not become at risk simply or solely as factors that exist within them as persons. To focus on only the student is to engage in victim blaming. In the looking at the school as an organization, the first concept I would like to discuss is organizational climate. I became interested in this concept after reading the infamous *Coleman Report* in 1966. What I learned was schools and classrooms that were open supported learning among the groups that Coleman et al. described as at risk. What my research found was that non-white males from low socioeconomic status and whose IQs were slightly below 100 made higher grades and had a better attitude toward learning than white females from upper socioeconomic status whose IQs were above 100, when they saw organizational climate including both the school and the classroom as open. The elements of the social climate scale include order, spontaneity, and support. The element which has held up the strongest over the past 25 years is order. Students learn best when they perceive that the teacher has control over the class and knows what is going on. The teacher is not out of control. This does not mean that the school or classroom is run by a principal or teacher through intimidation.

Schools must accommodate students by lengthening the school week and school day. This may be done with human service workers collaborating with teachers. The school is owned by the community. Hence, activities that the community wants should go on in the school during non-school hours. The school should become a centripetal force in the community where good things happen. If the community needs a laundromat, the school is an excellent place to put it.

The school is an organization. If it is to be an effective organization it must be cognizant of four organizational frames. They are bureaucratic, human resource, political, and existential. School managers that are effective pay attention to all four frames. The frame that is ignored is the one that will kill you. Briefly, these frames sensitize the manager to organizational roles, management by hanging around, and person as well as task management, conflict over scarce resources, and the importance of rituals. All of these are variables that are of crucial significance to organizations. Schools too often are run on a top-down model where collaboration is stifled. Organizations where communication runs both ways vertically ensures that the needs of faculty and students are more likely to be met than when communication is top-down only.

It is clear the problems of at risk students are more likely to be solved when both the role of the school and the student are examined and addressed.

Some Interventions That Show Promise

The following are a list of some interventions with a brief description that should be helpful to teachers and human service workers. (1) Conflict Resolution. Conflict resolution is a group activity that teachers may find useful. There needs to be a distinction however between school and community when conflict resolution is used. I tend to think that it will always be effective in a school setting but I am not so sure when it comes to the community. (2) The importance of culture cannot be overlooked. Almost all at-risk students have some unique cultural qualities that should be acknowledged in classroom activities. (3) Teachers must be taught the value of collaboration. General and special ed teachers must work together in a collaborative fashion. These teachers in turn must work with human service workers collaboratively. It is wise to remember that collaboration entails more than cooperation. A good beginning is coordination of services. (4) Agency is that little voice inside that says I can do it. It is something that teachers and human service workers can enable people to do and have. We can facilitate the development of that intrinsic voice. (5) Strain Theory states that the causes of social deviance reside within the place were the individual is, but where they do not want to be. If a person finds the school punitive and a place of constant failure they will do whatever they can to get out of it. Research on Hispanic males shows that their self concept rises dramatically when they leave school.

There are four groups of early school leavers. They are the quiet school leaver, those who act out overtly, those who compensate and quite often cheat, and those who persist but drop out of learning and may graduate illiterate.

Knowledge of these interventions should help in ameliorating the problem of at-risk youth in America today and in the future.

ENDNOTES

1. The interested reader is referred to Dryfoos' *The Full Service School* and Kronick's *They are Walking Around With Tombstones In Their Eyes*.
2. A full description of mental health needs of children is presented in Kronick and Hargis, 1998, *Dropouts: Who Drops Out and Why The Recommended Action, 2nd ed.*
3. See Charles Hargis for a full discussion of curriculum-based assessment.
4. See Kronick & Hargis (1998) for an in-depth discussion.

Chapter 6

APPALACHIAN STUDENTS AS AT RISK AND THE NEED FOR UNDERSTANDING THEM WITHIN A MULTICULTURAL FRAMEWORK

It is not unlikely that schools, more than any other arena, are the stage on which issues of cultural diversity are being played out in this society.

Spindler & Spindler (1993), p. 26

INTRODUCTION

TO MAKE MULTICULTURALISM HAVE MEANING beyond nothing more than a politically correct term, a definite behavioral definition with latitude is required. Multiculturalism and the concomitant respect needed for it must allow for many cultures to be included within it, not just those cultures that are "in" at any particular time. To understand multiculturalism, it is important to first understand the concept of culture. Culture is the potting soil for all behavior. It has been defined by the Spindlers (1993), as in process, in everything that we do, say, or think in or out of school. The concept of culture is so important to the Spindlers, that they have developed a notion of cultural therapy that they see as far more relevant for working with at-risk populations than personality theories. It is the Spindlers' contention that cultural therapy and anthropology have much more to offer human services than personality theories or psychology.

Cultural therapy focuses on the enduring self and the situated self. The enduring self has a sense of history and is rooted in our family of orientation. The situated self is contemporary and is faced with daily accommodations that the self must make in present actions. The enduring self makes compromises and accommodations constantly. At some point in time the negotiations between the situated self and the enduring self lead to the evolvement of the endangered self. The endangered self arises as a result of the negotiations that the situated self makes, where the resulting behavior is non-genuine and inauthentic. This tug-of-war between the enduring and situated self may help account for the resistance of some minority youth to learning in school or learning some aspects of what is being taught and accepting how it is taught. They may regard this as a sellout (Spindler & Spinder, 1993). Examples of this would include the Hispanic child who is told by his or her mother to respect the teacher and not look her in the eye. The Appalachian child who is too proud or too afraid of the stigma to ask for help. The Native American child who wrote the book on cooperative learning so well that teachers see them as cheaters. And the African American child who feels he or she must act white to achieve in school.

The Spindlers, in emphasizing the importance of culture and the self, developed a concept they call cultural therapy which they define as:

> A process of bringing one's own culture in its manifold form—assumptions, goals, values, beliefs, and communicative modes—to a level of awareness that permits one to perceive it as a potential bias in social interaction and in the acquisition or transmission of skills and knowledge. (1993, p. 28)

It is the Spindler's contention that one's actions can be taken as caused by one's culture and not by one's personality. They state:

> In our work with individual teachers we have found that the sociocultural position and experience of the individual is a better predictor of classroom behavior particularly in respect to selective bias on the part of teachers in perception of and interaction with students than psychological factors, such as indicated by psychological tests or interviews. (1993, p. 29)

In support of this finding, Kronick and Hargis (1990) found that high-status students in the classroom influenced the teacher not to call on low-status students. This was quoted by both high- and low-status students. This is a very sophisticated social psychological process but one that must be attended to by teacher training programs. It is clear that culture is far more operative here than personality. This finding argues the point cogently that stratification is at work within the broader, as well as the school culture. With all this in mind, the Spindlers state the goal of cultural therapy for students is to empower rather than to blame them. The concept of empowerment is at the heart of human service theory. It first of all forces us to move away from an ideology of victim blaming (Ryan, 1971). Empowerment facilitates full participation of all cultural groups in today's schools and society. It helps lead to a true valuing of a multicultural society. By making all parties responsible for their behavior, a giant step forward is made. The 1990s has seen the social creation of too many peoples being designated as victims. This victim category and role becomes all too comfortable for some. Another outcome of victim classification is that according to Ryan (1971) you can label these folks as less than human. When this is done any behavior no matter how heinous may be perpetrated on them. This becomes especially true for minorities, students and any persons without power. When looking at the relationship between the dominant culture and the other cultures in America, the Spindlers strongly assert "The problem in America and in American schools seems to be that in order to establish some kind of identity, mainstream American culture poses itself as dominant, supreme, moral, right, to be observed, and to be taught at all costs to everyone" (1993, p. 43).

Out of this interaction between the mainstream and other cultures emerges the individuals concept of self. The self emerges in various forms through the evolutionary states of development. Erickson (1963) discusses the development of trust vs. mistrust, autotomy vs. guilt, intimacy vs. isolation, and generativity vs. stagnation. Are these stages relevant for all cultures? Did Erickson take cultural difference into account when he developed these steps?

Charles Horton Cooley (1918) studied his own children in developing the concept of the looking-glass self. The looking-glass self says that we develop our sense of self from the reactions we get from other people. This concept is passive and looks as if the individual is nothing more than what society has made of him or her. Obviously this is not the case and the self like other social processes is more complex than this.

The concept which the Spindlers choose over the looking-glass self is instrumental competence. Instrumental competence for them is not passive and is defined by them as, "requiring that one understand what activities are linked to what goals and how to perform the activities (1993, p. 45). Self efficacy also is an active concept, and is an expectation that one exhibit instrumental competence in the appropriate context.

In following the Spindlers' model of the self discussed earlier, both instrumental competence and self efficacy are contextual in Spindlers expressions of the situated self. The situated self in its daily negotiation with others will struggle to perform with instrumental competence and to achieve a feeling of self efficacy. Children may fail in school because they do not master the competence of doing schoolwork. They may develop low self-esteem and low estimates of self efficacy in the school situation. In this type of situation they may even develop a failure syndrome where they fail at tasks that earlier they had succeeded in.

Because instrumental competence is contextual, school failure may be localized and the student may maintain a positive self concept in non-school settings, holding on to their enduring self. An example where the situated self is attacked in school is provided by Davidson and Phelan (1993), they report: "In one school we watched as the enthusiasm and hope of newly arrived immigrants gave way to a sober and skeptical view of their circumstances. As students encounter stereotypes about their abilities, assignments to low track classes, and adults who seem to have little time and even less inclination to assist them, the desire to succeed is tempered."

Appalachia as a Place and a Culture

Culture, cultural therapy, the self, both the enduring and the situated self, as well as the endangered self, are all found in Appalachia.

Appalachian culture, according to Best (1986) contains large doses of sensuousness, emotion and spirituality and promotes inductive reasoning, intuition, creativity and sensitivity in the arts. These characteristics of culture are not those of K through 12 education and put Appalachian students at risk. To further illustrate the counter position of Appalachian culture with mainstream culture is the cognitive-affective difference between them as seen by the differential use of guilt and shame. "Mountain people, as a rule, are more influenced by shame as a moral force than guilt"

(Best, 1986, p. 46).

The Appalachian people's behavior is far more affective than it is cognitive. "Thought for thought's sake is not a basic product of the culture. The product of thought is usually intimately connected with life as it is being lived by the person doing the thinking" (Best, 1986, p. 46).

Appalachia arguably is the poorest section of America today. In the 1960s, this fact was realized and one arm of the war of poverty was designed to bring the city to the country. The idea was to bring in a money economy and to get people who lived in the area to produce and consume, to become a part of the nation's Gross National Product. One way to do this was to build roads that go to these out-of-the-way places.

Roads were a major force in the war on poverty in the 1960s and this I saw from a personal perspective while working in one of the many war on poverty programs based in Appalachia. Thirty years later, *Appalachia* features an article entitled, *Appalachian Highways: Almost Home.* It was personally reinforcing to read this article and to see much that was perceived thirty years ago was accurate, and that roads as a central aspect of development in Appalachia was alive and well in 1996. In fact, according to this article, 76% of the highways that were begun in the 1960s were completed with 24% left to go. Interestingly enough the 24% remaining to be completed are going to cost more than the completed 76%. This is due to inflation, higher safety standards and planning costs. Baldwin (1996) reported that the time needed to complete a designated section of highway was 13 years. This time included planning, land acquisition, and construction. The most difficult highway sections to complete have often been saved for last.

As I personally observed thirty years ago, these highways were built to bring people into assessable locations rather than to accommodate existing traffic patterns. Baldwin (1996) quotes Appalachian Regional Commission Co-Chairman, Jesse White, as saying:

> Until communities and businesses have access to markets and resources, until workers are able to reasonably commute to jobs, and until patients can be within safe reach of doctors and medical care, the people of Appalachia will never have a full seat at the table of American prosperity. The Appalachian highways are more than roads in the mountains—they are very much a life line. (1996, p. 9)

Baldwin (1996) states that the roots of the developmental highway program are as old as the Appalachian Regional Commission itself. The President's Appalachian Regional Commission report of 1964 began by describing Appalachia as a region apart. It recommended that design and location of a developmental highway system should be A.R.C.'s first order of business. The report went on to say that developmental activity in Appalachia cannot proceed until isolation has been overcome.

There are several testimonials in Baldwin's article that economic success has occurred due to roads and corridors being completed in Appalachia. And there can be no doubt that progress has occurred since the 1960s. However, most outsiders can only guess at the amount of isolation even with television and other electronic advances that exist in Appalachia today. The research being done on family resource centers by Kronick and Stinnett (1997) attests to this. At the same time that progress can be seen on the economic front the same cannot be said for the educational scene especially in relative terms. The south and the Appalachian South are at the bottom of the list in terms of the measurement of the overall well-being of children (Kids Count, 1995), and at the top, for high school students leaving school before graduation.

Appalachia belongs in a multiculturalism based on diversity. It is characterized by its strong attachment to place, a sense of pride, a concern for being stigmatized and an affirmation that they would like to make things better for their children. Recent research, by Kronick and Stinnett (1997), found that Appalachian parents truly care about their children. The historical depictions of Appalachian families by Agee, along with photographs by Walker Evans, show Appalachian families in clapboard houses, poorly dressed, barefooted with worn pale faces staring off into space. These images often led to stereotypes that have become self-fulfilling prophecies. This process has a strong impact on Appalachian children while in school. The situated self of the Appalachian child is always under attack in the school setting. Often what this child knows is not valued in a school setting. What this child learns is often not valued or understood either. Best (1996) as quoted earlier describes the Appalachian child's style of learning as sensual. By this he means that they are right-brain learners, and students who are inductive. As mentioned earlier, this is not the dominant paradigm in K through 12 education today.

Chapter 7

COLLABORATION

Lisa Bloom
John Habel
Robert Kronick
Rebecca Lucas
Dorothy Stulberg

INTRODUCTION

MANY STUDIES, IN VARIOUS DISCIPLINES, have been conducted to establish the merits and benefits of collaborative research (Galinsky, Turnbull, Meglin, and Wilner, 1993; Crow, Levine, and Nager, 1992; Mendenhall, Oddou, and Franck, 1984; Endersby, 1996; Hafernik, Messerschmitt, and Vandrick, 1997). Benefits discussed include combined insight and wisdom, development of personal relationships, professional enrichment, increased efficiency, diverse perspectives and encouragement and support of colleagues. Some disadvantages are also cited. These include issues of power, failure to establish trust among collaborators, perspectives that differ about what it means to collaborate, and failure to invoke language common to all involved.

True collaboration does not occur effortlessly. Often when individuals come together with a common goal, they encounter barriers that threaten to subvert their efforts. Romer and Whipple (1991) describe barriers that exist in academic communities as being institutional (e.g., disciplinary divisions), physical (e.g., architectural or geographical

64

factors), or interpersonal (e.g., race or gender distinctions). Roles of authority and power can also pose obstacles to collaborative success.

This section of the chapter describes a collaborative group and examines the process of collaboration that takes place to determine real and imagined benefits and barriers. The benefits and barriers discussed are unique to this particular group, but could easily be described as common to any collaborative group. As one member stated, collaboration is like a "covered dish dinner where everyone brings two dishes; one with food to share" and an empty dish "to take food home in."

DESCRIPTION OF A COLLABORATIVE GROUP

I am involved in an interdisciplinary, qualitative research group that has been meeting over a long period of time in the College of Nursing at the University of TN-Knoxville. Group members include graduate students and professors from various academic disciplines—nursing, psychology, education, human ecology, and pre-medicineñ—and with medicine varying levels of research experience. Members of this group meet weekly for a period of two hours. During each meeting, an interview transcript is interpreted and analyzed for themes, using a phenomenological research methods and to share insights as they work collaboratively to solve research problems.

The research group has the reputation of being a non-hierarchical, non-threatening, collegial, scholarly group. The staying power of this particular group suggests that these researchers have devised a successful system of working together. In examining the collaborative process of this group, I intend to identify the virtues and vices of such a relationship.

Barriers to Collaboration

1. *Restricted Membership*

I learned of this group through word of mouth. Several of my colleagues and mentors suggested I attend a meeting in order to learn more about qualitative research. I was familiar with the group, but initially did not feel comfortable attending. The group was viewed by me, and possibly other graduate students and faculty, as an "elite club," attended by a few chosen intellectuals, but closed to the curious or less powerful. At no time did a group member vocalize this contention or even convey an unspoken message. This was simply an uninformed perspective of one graduate student. My perspective may be a common one to those interested in joining an already established group. Romer and Whipple (1991) might describe this as a barrier to collaborative success. This illustrates a potential problem of collaboration—collaborative relationships that are already established may be viewed as closed and intimidating by those on the outside.

2. *Power Status/Authority*

A second barrier to collaboration that is frequently discussed in the literature concerns power structure or levels of authority (Kail and Trimbur, 1987; Romer and Whipple, 1991; Hafernick, et al., 1997). Kail and Trimbur (1987) contend that an equal level of power among collaborators should characterize collaborative relationships. I question the feasibility of that contention. A group needs leadership—one or two individuals who take responsibility for the direction of the group. I would argue that any group assembled that has no leader, would only meet a short time before a leader emerges, a phenomena described by Shelly (1995) in his writings about group interaction. It seems more advantageous to the group, if they collaborate together to appoint someone to the position.

In the research group I attend, faculty members take the lead role in our interactions, with one professor holding more power than others do. The group meets informally, so there is no written description of the group makeup or identification of those in leadership positions. By the time I joined the group, these roles of status had been established for many years. I learned very quickly that certain group members held more power or authority than others did, simply by observing the group dynamics. I observed that graduate students defer to professors, more experienced researchers are quicker to comment on data, and that those new to phenomenolgy are more apt to struggle with the language involved, resulting in a sense of powerlessness. All of us are aware of our self-perceived status, as well as the status we place on others.

Shelly (1995) examines the "role of status and the honorific prestige accorded actors in groups" (p. 315). In his discussion of social interaction, he distinguishes between the emergent phenomenon in group behavior and a process of status generalization. Because the research group leader occupies a highly valued position in larger society, he is accorded the same status in the group. Status generalization takes place. Had the group come together as equals to find that a leader amoung them emerged as a result of the activity, the emergent phenomenon would have been illustrated. In this situation, status was accorded to the individual before formation of the group. He was expected to take the leadership role and continues to live up to that expectation.

3. *Oppression*

Hill-Collins (1986) writes about the interlocking nature of oppression. Is it possible that race, gender, and class influence the development of power structure within collaborative groups? Is it merely coincidence that the leader of my research group, composed mostly of females, is a white male? I rationalize that the leader gained that status as a result of his expertise in the area of research we are involved in. He has written extensively in the area and clearly speaks more authoritatively than others at times of confusion. Still, it is interesting to examine the multifaceted structure of power in groups when roles are interlocked, and the unavoidable resulting oppression. Traditionally, males have oppressed women, whites have oppressed blacks, and upper-class members of society have oppressed lower-class members. These lines of oppression can be drawn in nearly all relationships involving diversely composed groups.

In the research group under discussion, female faculty members may view male faculty members as having more power. It is possible that the language of interpretation used in the group intimidates new members, male and female. A second, potentially oppressed group is graduate students. Graduate students are intensely aware of their position along the continuum of power held in the group. No one wants to risk offending a professor or embarrass him/herself by making faulty statements in front of several professors. We carefully plan what and when we are going to speak in the group, never losing the awareness that our status is low on the power pole. Some student members have reported not feeling confident enough to speak in group meetings for several months after joining the group. In fact, it does take awhile to become acclimated to the language used in the phenomenological data interpretation process and many choose to "listen and learn" for several weeks, before feeling they have the "hang" of it.

There may be other barriers to the success of this collaborative group, but none seem to be inhibiting the process. I was initially intimidated by my inaccurate perceptions of the closed atmosphere of the group, but quickly found that the group welcomed newcomers and supported growth of the group. Through my own insecurities, I created a barrier that may or may not exist for others. A definite power structure exists for the group. While this may be a barrier, I think the knowledge possessed by the leader is invaluable to the goals of the group. In the leader, we have an authority on the type of research in which we are engaged. The final barrier discussed, oppression, may be the one true hurdle for the group to overcome. Unfortunately, I can't imagine how the oppressed can escape the oppression. The roles and status of women and graduate students have not changed in many years, and I don't think changes are forthcoming. While we may undergo changes in our self-perceptions, the perceptions of society are not likely to change. It is the societal perceptions that lead to states of oppression.

BENEFITS OF COLLABORATION

In order to describe the benefits and/or the drawbacks of this particular collaborative relationship, I would like to share the words of those involved in the relationship. A short, survey was conducted in the group and members were asked to identify the advantages/disadvantages of working collaboratively in the research group; to determine what attracted them to the group; to define "collaborative research"; and to describe other research group experiences and tell how they were similar or different.

1. *A Positive Experience*

In response to the query, "What, if anything, do you find particularly attractive about this group?" members responded with "fun and always exciting," "intellectually stimulating," "very enjoyable interactions:" and "I always look forward to going." The responses indicate that this experience is positive and one in which they want to engage. To this group, collaboration is a joint process, that is lively, supportive, and stimulating.

The survey revealed that group members came to know about the group from members already attending. Each member stated that another group member had invited him/her to the group. It is probably safe to say that those who receive invitations have some interest in qualitative research using phenomenological methods.

2. *Covered Dish Dinner*

Group members were also asked to define "collaborative research." While definitions varied, the responses held strong similarities and frequently illustrate the benefits gained in collaborating. Definitions include:

". . . research in which two or more people co-create new knowledge, one person doesn't set the agenda. . ."

"The whole is greater than the sum of its parts!"

". . . joint effort. . . with everyone on an equal playing field."

". . . people work together to solve a problem they both care about, although one. . . may care more than the other."

"Research conducted by. . . people. . . from different disciplines."

"Open exchange of thinking, views, and ideas resulting in the discovery of new knowledge using the research process and the group process."

And finally, this metaphor was offered:

"It's like a covered dish dinner where everyone brings two dishes; one with food to share and one empty to take food home in from everyone else's dish."

3. *Interaction And Diversity*

Advantages or benefits of this process, as identified by group members, have to do with interpersonal interactions and the diverse perspectives involved. In this group, interdisciplinary views and people in positions of varying status contribute to the richness of the data interpretation. In a collaborative relationship, there are multiple sets or eyes and ears working to interpret the data. Each "set" not only brings professional expertise learned in his/her discipline, but cultural biographies inform and enlighten individuals' perspectives, as well.

4. *Sharing And Support*

Another advantage of interaction involves the sharing and support that occurs. Group members talked about the sharing of ideas, the sharing of workload, and the sharing of self. In this type of research process, people share personal experiences that may be somewhat painful to share. When analyzing data of a delicate nature, members sometime identify with a particular experience and give others the benefit of that personal insight. Moments such as these bring the group together; resulting in a cohesive bond that didn't exist before. The bond or the relationship between group members produces a network of support that transcends many personal support systems. For graduate students actively working on a dissertation, this support becomes invaluable. Problems and concerns can be presented to the group for immediate deconstruction. The diverse perspectives may yield important insights to a problem clouded in confusion. More importantly to the graduate student may be the sustaining encouragement received by being part of the group.

PURPOSE AND DESCRIPTION

The purpose of this section of the chapter is twofold: (1) to contribute to the theoretical literature about the meaning of school-university collaboration and the building of adhocratic structures in the bureaucracy of the school, and (2) to ground this theoretical discussion in a description of the development of peer mediation practices among third graders in an elementary school located on a Native American reservation in a rural setting. During the past four years the collaborators—a regular classroom teacher, a counselor, and a director of special education, graduate students, and the authors, who are university faculty in psychology and special education—have engaged in a series of studies and action research about new practices at the school designed both to serve diverse students and to provide rich professional development opportunities for the collaborators. Among the projects in which we have been involved is "Peacekeepers" a comprehensive peer mediation program established across the third grade. Peacekeepers has been the subject of a masters thesis and has been presented at regional and national conferences.

Adhocracy

Our efforts to establish adhocratic structures at the school are based, in part, on the work of Skrtic (1995a, 1995b). Skrtic (1995a) characterizes schools as professional bureaucracies that are "premised on the principle of standardization" and "configured to perfect the practices that they have been standardized to perform" (p.202). Although these characteristics of schools reduce their ability to adapt to change and to innovate, schools, as public organizations, must respond to public demands for change. The most common way schools respond to change is by either adding subunits—programs and classrooms, for example—that require professionals with specialized knowledge or targeting teachers for endless inservice programs designed for giving prescriptions for effective teaching. These types of bureaucratic charges protect the organization from the need to actually change and clearly perpetuate the demarcation between research and practice.

Malouf and Schiller (1995) suggest that university researchers test new theories and practices via a linear model of research use. According to this model, research knowledge flows from university researchers to public school practitioners, who often are mandated to apply it regardless of its "fit." Typically, the practitioner's involvement in the process is limited to this post hoc application of research knowledge. Because research knowledge often is abstract and stripped of context, application typically is thin and veneer-like at best in classrooms and schools that are inherently unique in their circumstances. This linear model of research, despite its limitations, ends itself well to the traditional bureaucratic structure of schools and vice versa.

Alternatives to the linear model of research and the traditional bureaucracy of schools involve a number of approaches to: (1) reconceptualizing the roles of researcher and practitioner, (2) reducing the distinction between research and practice by focusing on the process as well as the outcome of research (Malouf & Schiller, 1995), and (3) attending to the experiential knowledge of the professional practitioners and giving them voice (Skrtic, 1995b).

The adhocracy emerges in an environment of uncertainty, innovation, and adaptation as an alternative to the bureaucracy (Skrtic, 1995a). Adhocracies are "premised on the principle of innovation" and function as "problem-solving organizations that invent new practices for work" (Skrtic, p.203) that is ambiguous and uncertain. Participants in an adhocracy cannot fall back on professionalization and specialization to divide work because ready-made, standardized practices do not exist for the work that is required. Therefore, the success of the work of an adhocracy depends on the ability of those involved to collaborate on an ad hoc basis on creative efforts to determine responses to "predicaments." Following the lead of Bruner (1983), we prefer to think of the behavior of collaborative groups in an adhocracy as "responding to predicaments," not solving problems. Use of the term "predicament" leads us to think of the demands of life, both professional and personal, as opportunities for growth and development rather than as problems to be avoided. In addition, one doesn't seek to solve a "predicament" once and for all; rather, one devises a response or series of responses. Situations where school professionals and university faculty collaborate to meet the needs of diverse populations of learners lend themselves well to an adhocratic structure and provide an alternative to linear research.

Adhocratic structures can promote school-university collaborations that bridge the gap between research and practice in public schools and contribute to the knowledge base of effective practices for educating diverse learners at all levels. By participating, teachers become integral parts of planning, implementing and evaluating practices. They can plan an important role in research, especially research that is non-linear. Teachers are no longer faced with the challenge of meeting the needs of diverse learners in isolation. Rather, as supportive groups of professionals meet, they can draw from various areas of interdisciplinary expertise to respond creatively to predicaments they face in their practice.

Collaboration

... a vision can die if people forget their connection to one another. ... Once people stop asking "What do we want to create?" And begin proselytizing the "official vision," the quality of ongoing conversation, and the quality of relationships nourished through the conversation erodes. One of the deepest desires underlying shared vision is the desire to be connected to a larger purpose and to one another. (Senge, p.230)

Adhocratic structures permit the question "What do we want to create?" to drive the practice of those involved. While this question does not necessarily supplant the "official vision" as a stimulus for behavior, it serves as a stimulus for innovation. In our efforts to establish adhocratic structures at the school, we have attempted to engage in a form of collaborative reflective thinking similar to that described by Schon (1987). Schon believes that while educators and other professionals can acquire essential professional knowledge from "packaged" professional principles delivered via credit-bearing courses, a second essential component of their learning comes through continuous action and reflection on everyday predicaments that they encounter in their practice. Schon holds that the information gained from this experience is often tacit and difficult to analyze. He does not refer to a cognitive knowledge base for teaching or other forms of professional practice; rather he refers to an "appreciation system." This system contains the professional's repertoire of theories, practices, knowledge and values which influence how situations are defined, what is noticed, and the kinds of questions and decisions one will form about particular actions.

Engaging in collaborative reflective thinking can help teachers organize and reflect on experiences in their practice (Henderson, 1992). This kind of thinking is meant to be a tool for teachers to generate a record of what they learn and what they think about the things they learn.

One purpose of the school-university group is to provide

relief from the isolation in which the members or the group often work. Teaching is an activity that both school and university educators almost always do alone. Collaboration (or collegiality) is a professional virtue; something that goes far beyond simple congeniality in the workplace or the classroom. When educators form a collaborative group, they can produce sense of community and shared commitment and a willingness to pool their energies, to share their burdens, and to complement one each other's strengths and weaknesses.

A second purpose of the school-university collaborative group is to provide those involved with opportunities to develop and refine their "appreciation systems;" to recapture experience in the field, to think about it, mull it over, and evaluate it. While unconscious processes of learning and/or teaching do occur, it is important that this activity take place at a conscious level. Unconscious processes do not allow one to make active and conscious decisions about our learning. It is only when one brings ideas to consciousness that one can evaluate them and begin to make choices about what one will and will not do.

A third purpose of the school-university collaborative group is to support participants' efforts to improve their own practice through action research. With both the school and the teacher as the units of change, action research projects focus on participants' actual predicaments while being grounded in the research-based literature that addresses the predicaments. This approach acknowledges that school goals and university goals coexist in the same context. The first step is for the participants in the school-university collaborative group to carefully identify one or more opportunities, circumstances, or predicaments that participants face in their practice at the school. Then they work collaboratively to describe the situation, generate one or more interventions, and establish procedures for evaluating these interventions. Action research is a form of inquiry that grants participants a research role based on a vision of the committed professional investigating his or her own practice (Carr and Kemmis, 1988).

When a school-university collaborative group is functioning well, there is a moral dimension to the kind of "shared vision" that members of the group strive to achieve. They view themselves not only as a collection of self-interested individuals driven by private goals, but primarily as a community of social individuals engaged in a search for shared meanings. Individual ends are intricately interrelated with the goals of their community, but the primary concerns are for the moral quality of the social relationships among the members of the team and for establishing and maintaining both shared initiative and mutual responsibility. Genuine collaboration in the public school in the service of children is a wonderful thing. Such collaboration has many dimensions, including : (1) good communication—mastering the practices of dialogue and discussion; (2) what Senge (1990) refers to as "operational trust," a condition in which individuals remain conscious of those with whom they collaborate and can be counted on to act in ways that complement their actions; and (3) learning how to deal creatively with powerful forces opposing genuine collaboration in organizations. In the school-university collaboration, these forces can be physical (the university and the school can be some distance from each other), institutional (individuals at the school can have views about complex and subtle issues that are very different from individuals at the other organization.

Peacekeepers

When we first met with a group of teachers, a counselor, and the director of exceptional children in Cherokee, North Carolina, the primary predicament we identified in meeting the needs of diverse learners was time to talk with each other.

As a result, we arranged for each grade block to have a planning day with a faculty member or a graduate student from the university as a facilitator. The role of the facilitator was to assist with brainstorming, taking notes and locating resources. The Peacekeepers came from a group of third-grade teachers, a special educator, a school counselor, and is described below.

A central theme that emerged from this first meeting was the need to develop a community within each third-grade classroom. The goal was to help children to be both respected and to be respectful. The teachers believed that if children felt some ownership of the procedures of their classrooms, then work habits and self-discipline would be improved. They also wanted the Peacekeepers to reflect the Native American culture of the school. The group determined that peer mediation might assist them in reaching those goals and drew ideas from professional literature, workshops they had attended, and their own experiences to develop their plan. The resulting philosophy and subsequent practices they developed within the third grade have been remarkably successful and have brought invitations to the teachers involved to present their ideas regionally, at the state level, and nationally.

In the third-grade classrooms, students are involved weekly in a council of peers aptly named Peacekeepers. Rituals and ceremonies involved with the Peacekeepers have helped develop a strong sense of community in the classroom. The structure of the Peacekeepers represents the local tribal council. Each week, the meeting starts with the recitation of the Peacekeepers' Pledge. An eagle feather, a sacred symbol according to Native American tradition, is passed from speaker to speaker, and the holder of the feather is the only one permitted to speak. A box is a central feature of a Peacekeepers' meeting; students and teachers have put compliments and concerns in the box throughout the week.

During each meeting, an elected chief reads each compliment after which the receiver of the compliment is applauded by the group. Concerns then provide an opportunity to engage in conflict resolution and the discussion of predicaments. Each concern is read and all parties involved are given an opportunity to tell their stories. Each member of the council is given a chance to suggest responses. Each response is recorded and then the group decides whether the response has been satisfactory or whether further action is needed.

The Peacekeepers also keep a basket of acceptance. This basket is placed in the center of the council and is filled with small objects from each member of the classroom. Each object reveals something about its owner. Objects have included things such as shells that one child collected on a special trip, a small token given to another child by his grandfather, etc. This type of ritual gives every child a chance to participate and symbolizes togetherness.

Community service is also an integral part of the Peacekeepers. The faculty and students decided that service was one way they could convey the spirit of the Peacekeepers to the larger community. Student-generated service projects have included cleaning the school restrooms, planting flowers in the community, and collecting canned goods for unemployed coal miners in Kentucky.

Each month all of the third-grade classes meet together for a Grand Council meeting. At each Grand Council meeting the chiefs for each grade give a report on the activities for their classrooms. These reports include concerns they have addressed and the progress they have made in resolving them. Updates about the status of community service activities are given.

Since the Peacekeepers were initiated almost three years ago, the philosophy and practices have spread slowly to other grades. The third-grade teachers have served as the conduits for this expansion. It is their hope that these practices will eventually permeate the entire elementary school.

Although the practices that have evolved from the initial Peacekeepers conception have not undergone rigorous empirical evaluation, a number of data-collection activities have been undertaken and documented. As part of a masters thesis, a graduate student interviewed both students and faculty about their experiences as Peacekeepers. Also, a log of all concerns, solutions attempted, and results has been maintained by the teachers. Third, the lead teacher in the third-grade conducted extensive interviews with the other third grade teachers regarding the Peacekeepers. Anecdotal records regarding children identified as behavior disordered have been maintained. Finally, a portfolio of the Peacekeepers including photographs and anecdotal records has been maintained. Following are excerpts from these various data sources.

A special education teacher reports that all of the teacher participants came together as a team to develop an effective intervention program for the children, and that the communication between regular and special educators has improved.

Another teacher shared a story about a child who is currently receiving special education services and is labeled behaviorally disordered. She states that at her initial Peacekeepers sessions he sat in the circle with head lowered during the entire session. When the children went around in a circle and attempted to assign strength words to themselves, his heartbreaking response was, "I am nothing!" With support from his community, he began to sit up and look around after about three council sessions. The teacher notes that since this uncertain beginning he has now become an active member of the community. She notes that he now speaks proudly at Peacekeepers meetings. Instead of passing when it is his turn to speak, he believes he has something valuable to contribute. His overall classroom work and behavior have improved as well.

One teacher shared a story of a student who was beginning to bully other children and often broke classroom rules. He applied for the position of chief and was elected in a secret ballot. The teacher noted the tremendous turnaround after the child took on the responsibility of chief; he has been seen complementing others and the complaints of bullying have stopped.

"Rightness" as a Source of Satisfaction

> . . . it makes no sense to assume that any powerful cognitive satisfaction springs from being told that one has done something right, as long as "rightness" is assessed by someone else. To become a source of real satisfaction, rightness must be seen as the fit with an order one has established oneself. (Glasersfeld, 1987, p. 329)

Our efforts to discuss the meaning of school-university collaboration and the building of adhocratic structures in the bureaucracy of the school and to ground this theoretical discussion in a description of the development of the Peacekeepers has become a source of satisfaction with sense or "rightness." The third-grade teacher who made the following remarks reveals this "rightness" in her life. "The idea of classroom councils or governments has been around for a while. All of us had read books, professional journal articles, attended workshops/seminars that encouraged the use of such practices. We as classroom teachers, had each in our own way incorporated many practices in our classes such as more choice and more use of cooperative learning across the curriculum that moved us nearer to the community/classroom council approach. I t was when we came together as a community of classroom teachers willing to work together and to discuss what was happening in our classes and ways to make it better that allowed us to take the next step to building strong communities. Our classes were missing something that we could not put our finger on but we knew that what was happening in our classrooms was merely on the surface, therefore, many solutions for problems in our classrooms were quick fixes, not truly meaningful changes that would last."

An Expert is One Who Gets Off an Airplane!

In October, 1998, Joy Dryfoos, author of *Full Service Schools* (1994) and *Safe Passage: Making It Through Adolescence in a Risky Society* (1998) visited The University of Tennessee, Knoxville. Approximately two hundred people attended her lecture which was given in our recently renovated College of Law. Those in attendance included faculty, students, and human service workers from the community and surrounding area. Some of the key points presented by Dryfoos were:

- Current services to children and families are fragmented
- The way to cut down on this is to create a seamless organization at the school where human services are delivered. The school is a neighborhood hub for services.
- This model adds to the learning of the students and makes the job of the teacher easier.
- A collaborative approach to clients is utilized by both teachers and human service workers.
- Management is bottom-up rather than top-down.
- Prevention and early intervention are stressed.
- The schoolhouse belongs to the community.

Among those in attendance that night was the Executive Director of the East Tennessee Community Services Agency. This person called me to say that he was very interested in what was said by Dryfoos that night. He said that he would like to bring together a group of his counterparts from upper East Tennessee, Middle Cumberland, and Chattanooga. These people are responsible for approximately 40 counties in this part of the state. Hence, our first meeting was held in Knoxville, Tennessee in mid-December to address what we had heard from Joy Dryfoos. The initial key points that this early version of the group was interested in was prevention and early intervention. At the end of the meeting, three key outcomes occurred:

1. We discovered that we were all on the same page in dealing with the delivery of services more efficiently and effectively for children.
2. Collaboration was our method of choice.
3. We would apply for some 21st Century After School Program grants administered by the United States Department of Education.

We also agreed that our group would continue to function after this particular grant deadline. We also agreed that in helping one another, we would not jeopardize our individual chances of securing a grant. As one member eloquently put it, "I haven't heard anyone say, `What's in it for me?'" This period of collaboration continues today. So far, four school systems from the collaborative have submitted grants to the 21st Century After School Program. A first meeting after the deadline for the grants is March 12, 1999. The groups' emphasis will change after the deadline. A more generic focus will probably evolve.

One focus that will evolve centers around the tobacco money that the state has been awarded. Most, if not all of the money, appears headed to the Health Department and Tenn Care, our state's version of welfare. It is our fervent hope to get some of this money for prevention, meaning preschool to elementary school. The 21st Century After School Program recast its focus from middle school only to include elementary school on February 1, 1999. This appears to be a major shift in emphasis as most prevention programs focused on middle schools.

COLLABORATION IN THE TENNESSEE CONSORTIUM FOR FULL SERVICE SCHOOLS

I have recently read two articles in the December, 1998 issue of *The American Educational Research Journal* on collaboration. I found these articles of absolutely no value. They give no clue on collaboration within professions. With the miserable delivery of services and their horrible fragmentation extant today, articles on collaboration must be clearly written and devoid of heavy language that is incomprehensible to those who want to move from cooperation to collaboration. Given my disappointment with these two articles in one of education's most prestigious journals, I will share some concepts that have emerged as the Tennessee Consortium for Full Service Schools evolves. It is important to remember that the consortium is in it's infancy and is in the process of developing.

I am sure that no one will be surprised when I say that the first step in our collaboration is communication. Our group is made up of academics and practitioners. Degrees range from BAs to Ph.D.s. Fields vary from Psychology, Political Science, Education, Child Development, and Social Work. Learning to speak the same language was our first task. Respect for competence, regardless of degree level, has come surprisingly easy. Nevertheless, communication is a critical component of collaboration and one that must be continually worked on. The key facet of communication is authority. Some of us are deemed more authoritative when we speak than others. Too often degree level is the reason for this.

The group has worked to see that all members are given equal voice. College students attend the consortium meetings and are treated with respect. What they say is seen as authoritative. We keep in mind constantly that communication is an issue which we must work on and practice.

A second element of collaboration is trust building. Human service workers are faced with developing trust among workers with clients all the time. It appears that as I enter the final stage of my career in human services, that I spend more time working with staff than with clients. The group members of the collaborative, over time, appear to be gaining trust. It would be naive to claim that this is 100 percent. Nevertheless, members are sharing valuable information with each other. As stated earlier, the philosophy of, "I give up or lose something by sharing it with you" is slowly giving way to "When I share, we all benefit."

Trust is a crucial element of this project to improve the overall well-being of children in Tennessee. If the providers are able to do away with turf issues, learn how to work together through communication and trust, all involved will benefit.

The natural evolution from effective communication and trust is clear agreements. After each meeting assignments are generally given to individuals from within the group. The academics are asked to share research articles, either their own or from the literature. Others have shared experiences or found grants that were submitted in earlier years to share. One of our practitioner members went to a training session in Atlanta, Georgia and brought back valuable information for the entire group. This person gave up her weekend to attend this workshop.

Along with communication, trust, and clear agreements, what else can we say about collaboration? Possibly the part of the country where we live is important. East Tennessee is, in many ways, a unique place to live. There are mountains, streams, valleys, gorges, beautiful land and lakes, and pollution. It is possible to be in a beautiful area, turn a corner and see garbage strewn everywhere. The mentality is my grand-father dumped here, well so can I. It is an area of many con-tradictions. There is little or no trust of government. From this follows a lack of trust of education. Hence, outsiders are looked upon with caution. Yet, outsiders, especially mine owners have taken advantage of these people. One must keep in mind that this is a generalization with exceptions. Most of East Tennessee is rural and even the cities in the area may best be seen as "urban". Knoxville is the largest city in the area and home to the state's land grant university. The university is known more for its athletics programs than it is for academics. With the exception of agriculture the campus has had little impact on the state especially when considering education, broadly defined, and human service issues. The state supports higher education as long as it leads to a job. It is from this environment that The Tennessee Consortium for the Establishment of Full Service Schools has evolved.

The consortium is an interesting mix of outsiders who have lived in Tennessee for 10 to 30 years, to people whose families go back several generations of being in the area. The outsiders are academics or agency administrations who all hold at least a master's degree. Two of the folk, one an academic, the other an agency administrator, have a twenty-five year history of working together. These two have collaborated on many projects involving edu-cation, corrections, and mental health. Some of the other members knew of each other but had not worked closely with much less collaborated with one another.

Thus, it is within this cultural milieu of individualism, I can do it on my own, individual volunteerism, remember this is the volunteer state so named for events in Texas a long time ago, that this collaborative is trying to exist and exert influ-ence for the children of this state.

Since The University of Tennessee is national champi-onship football this year, another facet of collaboration that we see as important is recognition. It almost seems self-evident that behaviors are strengthened and reinforced when rewarded, but so often we ignore this important dictum. We try to recognize and reward each member's contribution. By sharing with the group, these contributions may become even more viable.

The next important event for the collaborative is participating with Gloria Ladson-Billings author of *The Dream Keepers* on her visit to The University of Tennessee in April.

COLLABORATION MORE THAN COOPERATION

There are some key terms that must be identified both from a theoretical as well as a practical point of view when it comes to collaboration. Kronick and Hargis (1998) delineate cooperation, coordination, and collaboration as separate and distinct entities. By being aware of these distinctions, we are able to both identify as well as practice and to determine when, in fact, we are doing one when we might think we are doing another. For instance, quite often we think we are collaborating when in fact we are merely cooperating.

Crowson & Boyd (1996) list four external elements of collaboration: goal structures, institutional interests, environmental controls, and intellectual conventions. Goal structures are characterized by a shared control problem. Institutional interests revolve around the notion of reward structures. Environmental control illustrates how one of the collaborators may coopt the others. Institutional conventions concern themselves with rituals, stories, and ceremonies.

Collaboration has been defined by Lawson and Anderson (1996) as the sharing of common goals. A collaborative is a group who has agreed to be partners in addressing problems, in this case, school and human service problems. We are concerned with people who have problems in living. We do not want to see these people as problem people. Collaboration involves people from any areas who share power and work together to accomplish a goal. Collaboration requires partners to put aside their own agendas in favor of common goals. Collaboration is a mind-set that says, "I am going to need the help of others to do my job," Melaville and Blank (1993).

They further state that a group will know that it is ready for collaboration when all the parties realize that they have a shared problem that no one can solve alone and when they are ready to look beyond their interests to solve it.

A collaborative is a group who has agreed to be partners in addressing problems. Collaboration involves people from any areas who share power and work together to accomplish a goal, (Kronick & Hargis, 1998).

When mentioning the aspect of collaboration, one seemingly contradictory one is leadership. Leadership in a collaborative most likely follows the pluralist model of government. In the pluralist model, as the issue changes, those in leadership positions will change. This is termed by some as the transparent game of politics. For our purpose, this model helps us understand the role of leadership within a collaborative frame.

According to Crowson and Boyd (1996), services may run along a continuum from cooperation to collaboration. Cooperation involves individuals and organizations working together but having their own goals. Collaboration involves various individuals and groups working together and sharing a common set of goals. They further contend that most programs attempting to collaborate fall somewhere between cooperation and collaboration with the most common plan being colocation of services.

The following quote from the director of a Family Resource Center illustrates how cooperation/collaboration actually works. The reader may want to access where on the continuum of cooperation and collaboration this examples-falls. *"We found out that there are a lot of places that will pay for glasses and for some other needs of the kids; but they would not pay for the testing, for hearing tests and eye tests* (Kronick & Hargis 1998). So the Salvation Army decided that they would pay for that. So we have had some kids who have been able to get exams done through the Salvation Army. One of the things that came up, but it was after the school year had already started, so one of the units had already decided what their back to school program would be next year. There was also a member of the Health Department and she said as kids were coming through getting ready for kindergarten, they had to have their physicals. She saw how many kids did not have underwear. And, of course, already being in the school year, it was too late to go back and figure out who those were. She would be able to tell up front who those were and then through the school we can find some others. She will be able to target a whole lot of them at that point. So together we have been able to come up with some things and we are checking with parents to find out what their needs are rather than everybody else sitting back and dictating (Kronick & Hargis 1998). A sound conclusion to the burgeoning school of thought on collaboration is presented by Melaville and Blank (1993) when they state, although the stages of collaboration are incremental, progress often looks more like a spiral than a straight line, and partners must balance a focus on long-term goals with flexibility as they find the most effective ways to knit their local needs, resources, and preferences into a successful plan (p. 19). Ultimately, the successful implementation of collaborative agreements depends upon stakeholders collective ability to manage continuous change (Bradshaw 1998).

The Danger of Believing Two Plus Two Equals Four and the Joy of Knowing It Doesn't

There is prejudice in deterministic predictability. There is a new kind of knowledge (or a new way of learning) if we get out of our box and look around with our eyes and ears and self, ready to move past our fixed forms of thought. If we do, we will become aware of things we have never noticed, including our biases. There is a creative space between my thoughts and your thoughts and collaborative learning is the way of finding that creative space.

The words of the future (and of the past for those who have already moved out of the box) are chaos, non-linear, dynamical systems, phase space, differential equations, deterministic disorder, strange attractors, aperiodic behavior, fractals, complexity theory, complex adaptive systems, punctuated equilibrium, catastrophe theory. These words which are from a way of thinking, not expecting one solution, not working toward order but enjoying the complexity of life. "There is no single preexisting order to be discovered in our life or in our surroundings." Although the chaos theory came out of mathematics, it moved through physics, quantum mechanics, and on into the social sciences. Complex systems have the property that many competing behaviors are possible and the system tends to alternate among them. If we can understand dynamically how some of the complex features arise, it may be possible for society to understand itself leading to political resolution of dissension. Complexity is life itself and it is the foundation of collaborative learning. There is disorder if we are to create new knowledge. The results are not planned. There is exultation when arriving at a place never dreamed. There is a measureless complexity but thoughts and voice and dialogue weave and fold and spiral much like the beauty of the fractal curves. It is inquiry as a collaborative effort with people rather than investigation of them. It is socially constructing a relational society. It is a way to rational solutions instead of violence in settling the affairs of life. The disorder is followed by order but it is a different order than would have been possible before the thinking in the space between. The orders then followed by disorder.

There is beauty in the harmonious arrangement of order and disorder that is found in nature. So is there beauty in the harmonious arrangement of order and disorder in changing culture, in changing literature, in changing ways of teaching. And I propose, in ways of learning and thinking and living life.

I "came to" collaborative learning at the age of seventy when I began evening school at the University of Tennessee. I stumbled upon a new PhD program titled "Collaborative Learning." The students, called cohorts, are twelve in number and develop collaborative with the professors as equals, as having something to contribute. (The program has been criticized as not learning because the students are having too good a time. Imagine.) They must be working full time in a profession and be willing to apply to their practice, the new knowledge created in the space between. For me as a practicing lawyer, it meant the opening of new horizons, the disruption of habits and reconsideration of the law and the role of the lawyer. As I reflected on my practice and the law, I became aware of the unthought norm, the idea that I through my knowledge could solve someone's problems. By learning to learn, to reflect, to dialogue, to listen, I came to see what was already there, the "usually ignored." I moved off of my unawareness and into a whole new way of being. The present became alive, the past was reinterpreted, the future was full of excitement and potential and desirably unpredictable.

What it means to "come to" collaborative learning is a personal matter while at the same time it is "come to" only with and through others. Collaborative learning loses in description because it cannot be confined to words. It is something that is the very essence of being human. It is not easily reached but the striving for it is the learning. It includes reflecting on and recognizing one's assumptions, acting with the intent of opening opportunities so that everyone has the chance for the life they consider worthwhile, and, with others, thinking and creating knowledge which is new and not possible without collaboration. It is more than working together or cooperating or even collaborating with others. It is very special and does not come easily. Nor is it easy to define because, as one creates knowledge, so does one create a new and more exciting kind of collaborative learning. The collaborative process applies to the whole of life, it is in the practice that it becomes alive. *Collaborative learning is non-theoretical and is practice driven.* Attention is drawn to otherwise unnoticed features of our own conduct through a new way of talking and dialogue.

As a student, collaborative learning causes one to redefine one's responsibility toward the whole, toward education, the professors, the others, in fact to all facets of one's life.

Rom Harre finds the ultimate project of a human science is none other than the making explicit of knowledge of the third kind, knowledge that grows without participation in the acts of living. Collaborative learning is optimistic in a realistic way. We can by "looking" at what we do, by being in the moment, dialogue, hear and see and acknowledge the other and thus move on to new and higher forms of what it means to be alive and human. John Shotter sees the beginning of a politics of "identity" replacing a politics of power, a politics of access to or exclusion from a political economy of ontological opportunities for different ways of being. If one is to participate in this political economy with equal opportunity, then membership of the community of struggle, the tradition of argumentation, cannot be conditional: one must feel one has a right, unconditionally, to belong. The world faces new problems as we give recognition to the importance of differences. What questions will we ask? What relationships will be developed between students and faculty, among faculty and among students? How can power be shared? Through collaborative learning we have an opportunity to answer these questions with our violence.

Chapter 8

THE MOLLY STARK SCHOOL: A CASE STUDY

JOY DRYFOOS

Whether a youngster needs health services, social services, tutoring or simply after- hour activities, the school stands ready to provide it. In addition, Molly Stark's evening hour programs offer advice and counseling to parents as well.
Bennington Banner, Editorial, Feb. 4, 1998

THE INTRICATE INTERRELATIONSHIP BETWEEN healthy minds and healthy bodies has been known since the beginning of recorded history. We have been aware of the fact that the odds for academic success are much greater for children who are both mentally and physically sound. Schools' first role was to train little minds, and gradually over the ages we have added attention to the bodies: physical education, cafeterias, school health nurses, counseling, primary health clinics, along with a plethora of categorical prevention curricula. Drug and alcohol prevention, sexuality and family life education, violence reduction and behavioral modification, suicide prevention, nutrition enhancement, and even self-esteem workshops have all been loaded into schools in disconnected pieces of health education.

But it is only in recent times that "building" has been added to this equation. The environmental movement has raised our consciousness about the importance of toxic-free schoolhouses and the threat of violence has led to the call for

93

schools that are safe havens. And particularly in inner cities, we have schools that are bursting at the seams, some even collapsing from the pressure.

In communities without that tax base, the picture is quite different. School systems cannot afford to raise teachers' salaries and are struggling to reduce class sizes. In order to bring the three parts of the equation—mind, body, and building—together; outside help must be secured.

In my view, full service community schools bring together all three concepts into an integrated approach that places quality education and comprehensive support services in a building that enhances the experiences of the child and family early in the morning to late at night. That building serves as a neighborhood hub, an interesting and interested institution that is safe and comfortable.

THE MOLLY STARK SCHOOL

The Molly Stark School in Bennington, Vermont, is an excellent example of putting the pieces together. Here you will find a schoolhouse in the outskirts of a semi-rural community where the majority of the students are poor and have all the markers of struggling families and potential dropouts that are associated with big city life. These kinds of schools have low visibility in the national debate about raising standards and challenge the assumption that minority and big-city students are the ones with all the problems.

Five years ago, Sue Maguire took over as principal of the Molly Stark School, one where she had served as teacher and then assistant principal for 18 years. She was well acquainted with the problems in this school community that draws students from two large housing projects, six trailer parks, and other pockets of poverty. Test scores were low, excessive physical and verbal aggression was a major concern, and many students and parents were not committed to learning. In such an environment, the staff felt threatened, many of the children failed to learn (and eventually dropped out), and the parents rarely showed up. Maguire knew that planned action was required and set about reorganizing the school.

Changing the Outlook

At the outset, school staff, parents, and community agency representatives were brought together in focus groups to conduct a needs assessment and generate ideas about how to proceed. Over the past four years, a transformation has taken place and Molly Stark has become a model of a full-service community school, implemented by school people in partnerships with outside community agencies. This school building has expanded both physically and ideologically, adding a Family Resource Center to accommodate early childhood and parent programs, and changing the whole school into a challenging, stimulating, and welcoming environment.

The philosophy that governs this school is child and family centered. An important goal is to strengthen families capacities to support their children educationally, socially, physically, and emotionally. To accomplish this requires a comprehensive array of educational, health, and social services, what is described as "a holistic approach to student and family services."

Molly Stark today calls itself A Community of Learners. It has 415 preschool to 6th grade students with very diverse characteristics. About 54 percent are from poverty families and 22 percent are designated special education. The school is open all day from 7am till 5:30pm, with a substantial after-school program that includes more than half of the students.

Programs and Services at Molly Stark

The list of more than 50 activities (Table 1) fall into four categories: social responsibility, curriculum/instruction, family involvement, and wellness. A few are school-district-wide programs while most are unique to this school. Several are described in detail.

Table 1
Current Initiatives at Molly Stark School

Social Responsibility
Closed circuit TV
Mentoring
Primary Project
Continuum of interventions regarding behavior
Planning room
Conflict resolution training
Student conflict managers
At-Risk support groups
Adventure Education
School store
Peer tutoring

Curriculum Instruction
Early Education Program: Integrated Pilot Pre-school
Coordination of Title 1 and SPED services
Instructional Support Team
School-wide focus on reading
school-wide running records assessment
After school enrichment clubs
Homework/study skills clubs
Phonological awareness for all kindergartners
Before school and after school reading services
Math Olympics program
Molly Stark scholarship
Golden Pencil Program and Artists in Residence
Academic Summer Camps
Odyssey of the Mind Program
Thinking Cap Quiz Program

Family Involvement
Child care: before and after school, vacation and summer
Kindergarten child care
Home-school partnership
Kindergarten parent connection program
Play groups for parents with infants and toddlers
Newsletter
Recreational/educational family nights
Parenting classes
Open house/school-wide picnic
Parent/teacher goal setting conferences
Parent volunteers
Bagel bashes with parents
Kindercamp
Adult education
Parent Outreach Program
Literacy activities for family with lending library story hours

Wellness
PHASE (Promoting Health and Supporting Education)
   Team includes psychologist, pediatrician consultants
Healthy snack cart
Breakfast program
Well physicals and inoculations, including pre-schoolers
Staff flu shots
Wellness program for staff
Health fair
Social worker
Dental program
Health and nutrition for parents

Early Intervention

Molly Stark's plan addresses early childhood through literacy programs, playgroups for parents and their children, and parent educators who work with the parents both at school and in their homes. Screenings for early detection of health and learning problems are available in the Family Center. Kindergarten Child Care is offered to extend the kindergarten experience to a full day.

After School Programs

Some 22 different programs are offered after school in eight-week sessions. About 220 students sign up for these mini-courses and their parents pay a minimal fee of $4 per eight-week program. The variety of courses is broad, and changes with whom are available to teach. In addition to homework and reading clubs, students can take Tai Kwon Do, cooking, arts, auto mechanics, computers, sign language, foreign language, rock and roll band, gardening, etc.

The Family Center is a licensed child-care facility, with school-age child care before and after school, and through the summer.

Parent Involvement

This school places high priority on active engagement of parents. After the child enters school, the parents are encouraged to participate in parent support groups, parenting classes and home visits. GED and "Read With Me" classes teach parents to share books with their children. A lending library of books and educational games is available to all. The Community College of Vermont offers classes to parents at the Family Resource Center.

Mentoring

The PALS program is similar to Big Brothers/Big Sisters. Local high school students receive community service for mentoring a Molly Stark student. In another mentoring program, employees from local businesses spend one hour of their work time every week in the school with a student.

Health Services

Local physicians provide immunizations and well-child physicals for all 3rd and 6th graders as well as a dental program for children who do not have private care. A local pediatrician and psychologists are one site one day per week for short-term interventions and referral. Partners include the Southwest Vermont Medical Center and the Vermont Department of Health.

Governance and Funding

Molly Stark community school is operated by the school system. It relies on the presence of a strong principal, with most of the initiatives generated from inside the school. Many partnerships have been established with community agencies to augment services and programs run by the school (see Table 2). Regular and frequent gatherings are held that foster communication among the school team and between the school team and the partner-providers. In addition to formal meetings, the principal and the team members follow an "open door" approach encouraging everyone in the school community to participate.

Table 2
Partners With Molly Stark School

Sunrise Family Resource Center

Community College of Vermont
Headstart
Career Development Center from Bennington High School
Southern Vermont Community College
Bennington Family Practice
Big Brothers/Big Sisters
United Counseling Service
Local pediatricians, psychologists, and dentists
Local businesses

One impetus for this comprehensive approach has been new flexibility in funding. Several years ago, changes in Title I funding (federal funds for disadvantaged children) allowed the money to be used for school-wide programs rather than traditional remediation classes. As a result, this school has been able to use its Title I funding to develop a more comprehensive approach to enhanced learning.

Initially, the school became affiliated with the Schools of the 21st Century group at Yale University, and initiated a number of early childhood interventions. More recently, Molly Stark staff has turned to the Harvard Collaborative for Integrated School Services for technical assistance. Staff has also received training in Parents as Teachers, a national model.

In 1999, the Family Center grant of $291,000 was awarded to Molly Stark from the Vermont Community Development Block Grant Program to build a 3,600 square foot addition to the school. Vermont Governor Howard Dean and Lt. Gov. Doug Racine have been very supportive and look to this school to serve as a model for the state. The building is leased to the Sunrise Family Resource Center, a Molly Stark partner, for $1 a year, to prevent the space from being converted into classrooms at a later date. The school system takes responsibility for operation and maintenance.

The Molly Stark School receives $6,495 per child from the Bennington school system. In addition, Maguire actively pursues funding for all the different pieces of this program from federal, state, and private groups such as the Children's Trust Fund, the Vermont Council of Humanities and other foundations. As a result, grants from many different sources support diverse activities; some grants are for three to five years. It is hard to separate out the yearly costs added on by full services. In the 1998/99 school year, the total was about $68,000, with approximately $165,000 expected for 1999/00, plus an additional $291,000 for a building.

Evidence of Success

Molly Stark embodies the mind, body, building equation. Over the past four years, the entire school climate has been turned around. A visit to the school reveals a stimulating atmosphere with strong emphasis on graphic arts. The walls are covered with imaginative student work that gives the school a pleasing and welcoming ambiance.

The staff reports a discernible decline in physical and verbal aggression. The school has collected data on test scores, reading growth, discipline, attendance, parent support and involvement, family self-sufficiency, and other factors. Preliminary analyses show positive results. A significant improvement in academic achievement has occurred; 63 percent of students met standards in reading last year, up from 41 percent in a previous year. The school experienced a marked decrease in suspensions and a slight decrease in absenteeism. The staff noted great success in encouraging parent participation in parent/teacher conferences (from 59 students who were not represented to 3). A more formal evaluation is now being conducted through the Harvard Collaborative.

Implementation Issues

Targeting?

What is the purpose of opening the school doors for extended hours? Is it to supplement the lives of disadvantaged children or to enrich the experiences of children from every socioeconomic group? According to Sue Maguire, ". . . if you are making school-wide change, it is good for all kids not just one group." She cites an example of the many school-wide enrichment programs that have been instituted that challenge all students and provide a broad array of opportunities. The community school addresses the needs of all learners and all families and tries to address them "where they are" and respond accordingly. The staff believes that all parents need help at some time to bring up their children in this society.

An interesting unanticipated effect of developing this full-service school has been large number os advantaged students from outside of the school neighborhood who have transferred to Molly Stark. Their parents are drawn not only by the opportunity for parent involvement, but also because of the enhanced learning climate that they believe will enrich their children.

Continuity?

An energetic and committed principal has initiated much of this activity. The success of the school lends testimony to her leadership abilities. The responsibility for these many programs is shared with a coordinator of the Family Center and an assistant principal. If the current principal left, it is possible that one of these people could succeed her, or the system would need to find someone with a similar philosophy and plenty of energy.

The Future

The Molly Stark School after four years of development has emerged as a model for the state (and potentially for the country). In the fall of 1999, Vermont's Lieutenant Governor, Douglas Racine, convened a daylong conference on full service community schools, using Molly Stark as a "home grown version of this effort to integrate education with other programs for children. . . . Taking advantage of various community resources, such as the local parent/child center, adult education, health care providers, businesses, and many others, Bennington's Molly Stark School has coordinated and developed a broad range of services all aimed at helping families help their children succeed." The state of Vermont appears to be ready to communicate these ideas to other schools and to encourage and plan a network of full service community schools across the state.

National Significance

The experience of Molly Stark mirrors what is happening around the country. The idea of combining quality education, support services, parent involvement, and community development is rapidly gaining ground in many different versions. A Coalition for Community Schools now includes more than 100 national education and social support organizations.

Chapter 9

CONCLUSION

BRILL PRESENTS A MODEL OF STEPS IN THE problem-solving process of a human service team. The model is composed of the following steps: (1) problem, (2) purpose, (3) goals, (4) tasks, (5) roles, (6) interventions, and (7) evaluation and revision (Brill, 1998, p. 203).

EVALUATION AND REVISION

Team
Decision

are continuous and ongoing in each step of the process and are a part of the total process. From here, team can return to beginning or any point in progression fro revision.

INTERVENTION

Team and
Specialist Decision

is the enactment of roles through task performance, leading toward achievement of goals, realization of purpose, and problem solution.

ROLES

Team and
Specialist Decision

are defined according to specific assigned responsibilities for task performance.

TASKS

Team and
Specialist Decision

are specific work undertakings, on performance of which goal accomplishment depends.

GOALS

Team Decision

are specific ends that, when achieved, serve as progressive steps toward realization of purpose.

PURPOSE

Community, Organization, and Team Decision

is the designation and provision of service to solve the problem.

PROBLEM

is the involving need for maximization of human potential, prevention of human breakdown, or remediation of human suffering.

This model is a perfect illustration of how the Tennessee Consortium for the Development of Full Service Schools has gone about attempting to establish full service schools in Tennessee. Problem has been defined as the need to (1) cut down on the number of early school leavers, (2) increase learning, (3) meet the non-curricular needs of children and families that attend the school. The steps that are involved here include prevention, remediation, and maximization. It must continually be remembered that full service schools are for all children.

The purpose of the full service school is to solve problems as defined by the children, families, and school personnel.

The goals are empirical and can be measured. They include attendance, grades, conduct, health, mental health, and decreased involvement with juvenile corrections.

The tasks are specific work undertakings that lead to successfully reaching the goals. They include examining attendance records of each child, pulling grades from grade sheets, interviewing teachers about the child's conduct, checking health and mental health needs with school nurses, public health officials, pediatricians, et al., and examining the child's record for involvement with the law. Interviews with corrections and mental health professionals will be incredibly valuable.

The roles of those involved with the project will be defined along a specialist generalist continuum. The individual professional's expertise will shape their role in the project. Based on competence and/or degree individuals will go through attendance records and grades, check involvement with health and mental health as well as corrections and referral to the principal for behavior problems.

The intervention is the establishment of full service schools. This will lead toward achievement of goals, realization of purposes, and solving problems. A comparison with control schools that are not full service will lead to evaluation and revision if necessary.

Evaluation will tell how well we are doing. The concepts define the problems that are operationalized concretely and measured. At the level of process evaluation changes may be initiated so that needed changes may be instituted. Finally, an outcome evaluation will be done to determine the effectiveness of the project.

The time for the full service school is now. Some programs like Beacons in New York and Molly Stark in Vermont are a good beginning. Let's have a systemic set of full service schools in America, the alternative is too high a price to pay.

REFERENCES

Alinsky, S. (1972). Rules for Radicals. New York: Vintage Books.

Astor, R., Meyer, H., & Behre, W. Unowned places and times: Maps and interviews about violence in high schools. *American Educational Research Journal.* Vol. 36, No. 1-Spring 1999.

Bradshaw, L. (1998). Down East Collaboration. Paper presented at Brill, N. (1998) Working With People (6th ed.). New York: Longman.

Baldwin. F. (1996), Appalachian highways: Almost home but a long way to go. *Appalachia,* Volume 29, Washington, DC: Appalachian Regional Commission.

Best, B. (1986). *The great appalachian sperm bank and other writings.* Berea, KY: Kentucky Imprints.

Betts, E . (1946). *Foundations of reading instruction.* New York: American Books.

Bolman, L., & Deal, T. (1997). *Reframing organizations: Artistry, choice, and leadership.* San Francisco: Jossey-Bass.

Brill, N. (1998). *Working with people: The helping process.* New York: Longman.

Bruner, J. S. (1983). *In search of mind: Essays in autobiography.* New York: Harper & Row.

Burgess, E. (1927). *The urban community. Chicago:* University of Chicago Press.

Calfee, C., Witmer, F., Meredith, M. (1998). *Building a full service school.* San Francisco: Jossey-Bass.

Carr, W., & Kemmis, S. (1988). *Becoming critical: Education, knowledge, and action research.* Philadelphia: The Falmer Press.

Coleman, J. et al. (1966). *Equality of educational opportunity.* Washington, D.C.: United States Printing Office.

Collins, P. H. (1986). Learning from the outsider within: The sociological significance of black feminist thought. *Social Problems,* 33 (6), S14-S31.

Combs, A. & Snygg, D. (1959). *Individual behavior.* New York: Harper.

Comer, J. (1996). *Rallying the whole village.* New York: Teachers College Press.

Cooley, C. (1981). *Social process.* New York: Charles Scribners Sons.

Crow, G. M., Levine, L., and Nager, N. (1992). Are three heads better than one? Reflections on doing collaborative interdisciplinary research. *American Educational Research Journal,* 29 (4), 737-753.

Crowson, R., & Boyd, W. (1996). Structure & strategies toward an understanding of alternative models for coordinated children services. In J. Cibulka & W. Kritek (Eds). *Coordination among schools,*

107

families, & communities. pp. 137-172. Albany. State University of New York Press.

Davidson, A., & Phelan, P. (1993). Cultural Diversity and its implications for schooling: A continuing American dialogue. In P. Phelan and A. Davidson (Eds.), *Renegotiating cultural diversity in american schools* (pp. 2-15). New York: Teachers College Press.

Deci, E. L., & Ryan, R. M. (1991). *Intrinsic motivation and self determination in human behavior.* New York: Plenum Press.

Dryfoos, J. (1994). *Full service schools: A revolution in health and services for children, youth, and families.* San Francisco: Jossey-Bass. American Research Association Annual Meeting April 1998. San Diego, CA.

Dryfoos, J. (1998). Safe passage: *Making pt through adolescence in a risky society.* New York: Oxford University Press.

Endersby J. W. (1996). Collaborative research in the social sciences: Multiple authorship and publication credit. *Social Science Quarterly, 77* (2), 375-392.

Erickson, E. H. (1963). *Childhood & society,* (2nd ed.) New York: Norton.

Eysenck, H. (1952). The effects of psychotherapy: An evaluation. *Journal of Counseling Psychology* 16, 319-324.

Faris, R., & Dunham, H. (1966). *Mental disorders in urban areas.* New York: Hafner Pub.

Fuller, H. (1996). Revolution, not reform: Only radical transformation of U.S. education will serve neediest children. *Journal of Public Service and Outreach.* Athens, GA: University of Georgia.

Galinsky, M. J., Turnbull, J. E., Meglin, D. E., & Wilner, M. E. (1993). Confronting the reality of collaborative practice research: Issues of practice, design, measurement, and team development. *Social Work,* 38 (4), 440-449.

Gault In Re 387 U.S. 1, 87 S.Ct. 1428.

Glasersfeld, E. (1987). *The construction of knowledge: Contributions to conceptual semantics.* Seaside, CA: Instersystems Publications.

Hafernik, J. J., Messerschmitt, D. S., and Vandrick, S. (1997). Collaborative research: Why and how? *Educational Researcher,* 26 (X), 31-35.

Hargis, C. (1987). *Curriculum based assessment: A primer.* Springfield, IL: Charles C Thomas.

Henderson, J. G. (1992). *Reflective teaching: Becoming an inquiring educator.* New York: McMillan.

Higgs, G., & Tarsi, N. (1997). New learning and coping in the at promise student. In R. Kronick (Ed.), At risk youth: Theory, practice, and reform. New York: Garland Press.

Kids Count (1995). Baltimore, MD: Annie E. Casey Foundation.

Kronick, R. (Ed.). (1997). *At risk youth: Theory, practice and reform.* New York: Garland Press.

Kronick, R., & Hargis, C. (1998). *Dropouts: Who Drops Out & Why & The Recommended Action.* Springfield, IL: Charles C Thomas.

Kronick, R. (1999). They're walking around with tombstones in their eyes. *Human Services in the 21st Century. Council For Standards in Human Services Education.* McClam & Woodside (Eds.).

Lawson, R., & Anderson, P. (1996). Creating community collaboration: families, schools, communities, & higher education, pp. 161-172. In Harris, H. & Maloney, D. *Human services: contemporary issues & trends.* Boston: Allyn & Bacon.

Lawson, R., & Anderson, P. (1996). Community based schools: Collaboration between human services & schools as radical educational reform. In Harris, H., & Maloney, D. (Eds.) *Human Services Contemporary Issues & Trends.* Boston, Allyn, and Bacon.

Lewin, K. (1951). *Field theory in social science.* New York. Harper.

Malouf, D. B., & Schiller, E. P. (1995). Practice and research in special education. *Exceptional Children,* 61, 414-424.

Melaville, A., & Blank, M. (1993). Together we can: A guide for crafting a profamily system of education and human services. Washington, DC. U.S. Department of Education & U.S. Department of Health and Human Services.

Mendenhall, M., Oddou, G., & Franck, L. (1984). The trend toward research collaboration in social psychological research. *The Journal of Social Psychology,* 122 (1), 101-103.

Moos, R. (1970). Differential effects of the social climate of correctional institutions. *Journal of Research and Crime and Delinquency,* 7, 71-82.

Park, R., Burgess, E., McKenzie, R. (1967). *The city.* Chicago: University of Chicago Press.

Parlin, A. & Grew, K. (1996). Human services in the schools: History & focus, pp. 151-160 In Harris, H. & Maloney, D. *Human services contemporary issues & trends.* Boston. Allyn & Bacon.

Rumberger, R., & Larson, K. (1994). Keeping high risk Chicano students in school. In R. Rossi (Ed.), *Schools and students at risk.* New York: Teachers College Press.

Romer, K. T., & Whipple, W. R. (1991). Collaboration across the power line. *College Teaching,* 39 (2), 66-70.

Ryan, W. (1976). *Blaming the victim.* New York: Random House.

Schon, D. A. (1983). *The Reflective practitioner.* New York: Basic Books.

Schon, D. A. (1987). *Educating the reflective practitioner.* San Francisco: Jossey-Bass.

Senge, P. M. (1990). *The fifth discipline: The art and practice of the learning organization.* New York: Doubleday.

Shelly, R. K. (1995). Extending interaction theory. *Small Group Research,* 26 (3), 315-327.

Shotter, John. (1993). *Cultural politics of everyday life, social constructionism, rhetoric and knowing of the third kind.* Buckingham: Open University Press.

Skrtic, T. M. (1995b). Deconstructing/reconstructing public education: Social reconstruction in the post modern era. In T. M. Skrtic (Ed.) *Disability and democracy.* pp. 233-273, New York: Teachers College Press.

Spindler, G., & Spindler, L. (1993). The process of culture in person: Cultural therapy and culturally diverse schools and renegotiating cultural diversity in American schools. In P. Phelan and A. Davidsion (Eds.), *Renegotiating Cultural Diversity in American Schools* (pp. 27-50). New York: Teachers College Press.

Taylor, S., & Bogdan, R. (1984) *Introduction to qualitative research. The search for meaning.* 2nd Ed. New York: John Wiley.

Thomas, W. I. (1967). *The unadjusted girl.* New York. Harper & Row.

Tyack, D. (1992). Health & social services in public schools: Historical perspectives. *The Future of Children* 2(1), 19-31.

INDEX

DATE DUE

GAYLORD			PRINTED IN U.S.A.